Religion in Korea

Harmony and Coexistence

KOREA ESSENTIALS No. 10

Religion in Korea

Harmony and Coexistence

First Published in 2012 by Seoul Selection
B1 Korean Publishers Association Bldg., 105-2 Sagan-dong,
Jongno-gu, Seoul 110-190, Korea
Phone: (82-2) 734-9567
Fax: (82-2) 734-9562
Email: publisher@seoulselection.com
Website: www.seoulselection.com

ISBN: 978-89-97639-05-2 04200
ISBN: 978-89-91913-70-7 (set)
Printed in the Republic of Korea

Religion in Korea

Harmony and Coexistence

KOREA FOUNDATION
한국국제교류재단

Seoul Selection

CONTENTS

Appendix

Delving Deeper

Introduction

Korea is a remarkable case study in religious coexistence.

Even though only about half the country identifies as religious, the half that does displays a remarkable diversity of both indigenous and imported faiths, including Buddhism and Christianity (of both the Catholic and Protestant varieties). What is even more amazing is the extent to which faiths seemingly overlap: even the avowedly non-religious participate in shaman rituals, Buddhist temples host shrines to Taoist spirits, and it would be no exaggeration to say that Korean society—regardless of professed faith—is based on a bedrock of Confucian norms so solid the nation is often called the most Confucian country on Earth.

Korean religious pluralism is no recent phenomenon. Koreans have respected religious diversity since ancient times. Indeed, if there is one overriding religious tendency in the Korean population, it is a preference for syncretism, seeking essential and common truths amidst diverse and often competing doctrines. Current Korean leaders have continued making efforts to further inter-faith understanding. The Korean Council of Religious Leaders, an organization composed of senior leaders from Korea's major faiths, meets regularly to promote mutual understanding and tolerance. It also stages an annual Republic of Korea Religious Culture Festival, a public event aimed at promoting reconciliation and understanding.

This book surveys the rich religious and spiritual tapestry that is contemporary Korea. We begin with the earliest of Korean faiths—the shamanism that prehistoric Koreans brought with them as they migrated to the peninsula from Central Asia—and continue on to today's most prominent faiths: Buddhism, Christianity, and Confucianism. Korea has given birth to a large number of indigenous faiths, and we will take a look at some of these, too.

In examining each faith, we will look at both their basic beliefs and the unique styles that these faiths developed in the Korean cultural context. Each chapter will also include short "sidebox" articles on especially relevant or interesting figures, events, and concepts associated with the faith in question. These not only make the volume a more enjoyable user experience, but also help the reader gain a deeper understanding of Korea's religious history and environment.

We must add one caveat, however: this volume should not be regarded as definitive. Korea has proved fertile religious ground, with countless faiths present in the country. Due to space concerns, we could not hope to include each and every one. This practical decision should in no way be taken as a statement on the value or importance of the excluded faiths.

"Korea provides a particularly fruitful laboratory for the study of spirituality in the modern world because of the great variety of religious, philosophical, and spiritual beliefs and practices found here. Korea offers its people a wider range of spiritual and religious techniques for addressing the problems of life than do countries such Italy and Pakistan that have a single dominant religion. Koreans can choose from polytheist, monotheist, or nontheist conceptions of invisible powers greater than themselves. They can seek solutions to the difficulties they encounter through prayer, meditation, study, chanting, somber ritual, or playful interaction with gods and spirits."

Don Baker,
Associate Professor, University of British Columbia
Korean Spirituality, 2008

1 Chapter One

SHAMANISM

The word “shamanism” derives from the Tungustic languages of eastern Siberia, with the term “shaman” itself referring to the priests of the Tungustic tribes. Defining shamanism has long been a tricky matter, and a great deal of scholarly debate has centered on determining just what it is. Most definitions, however, focus on the role of the shaman, a religious figure who, by entering into trances and other ecstatic states, plays the role of bridge between the earthly and spirit realms.

In his essay “What Is Korean Shamanism?” Korean shamanism scholar Kim Tae-gon defines shamanism as “a traditional, religious phenomenon tied closely with nature and the surrounding world, in which a practitioner endowed with the special ability to enter a state of trance-possession can communicate with supernatural beings. This transcendental power allows the practitioner, the shaman, to satisfy human cravings for explanation, understanding and prophecy.”

Shamanism is best known its in its Siberian, Asian, and Indigenous American incarnations, but beliefs and practices were, and in many cases still are, in evidence virtually worldwide.

In Korea, shamanism (*musok* or *mugyo* in Korean) was the preeminent religious belief prior to the arrival of Buddhism on Korean shores in the Three Kingdoms Period (57 BC–AD 668). Even after the widespread adoption of Buddhism, however, it continued to have a great impact on spiritual life, both as its own set of beliefs and practices and through its impact on Korean Buddhism, which adopted a number of shamanistic practices. This trend would continue even after the adoption of Confucianism as a ruling philosophy at the start of the Joseon Dynasty and, still later, survive the introduction of Catholicism and Protestant Christianity.

The great shaman Lee Hye-gyeong holds a Hwanghae-do *sinsa maji gut*.

The 20th century was largely unkind to shamanism, which faced repression at the hands of both Korea's Japanese colonial overlords and, following Korea's liberation from colonial rule, Korea's modernization-focused military dictators, who viewed it as an embarrassing holdover from a backward past. A combination of democratization, economic development, and growing pride in Korean traditional culture, however, has helped bring about a revival, and the faith remains an important source of spiritual wisdom and comfort for many Koreans today.

(Left) *Jangseung*, totems placed at the entrance of a village to drive away evil spirits
(Right) A *gosa*, a shamanist rite in which food is offered to the gods in hopes of bringing prosperity and good luck. These are often held when moving to a new home, starting a new business, buying a new car and other ventures.

HISTORY

Nobody knows for certain when shamanistic practices began. Evidence in the form of cave drawings suggests shmanistic beliefs and practices date back to the Neolithic and Paleolithic Ages. Shamanism particularly flourished on the steppes and forests of Siberia and Central Asia, where the harsh climactic conditions and the nomadic lifestyles of its peoples encouraged a strong respect and reverence for nature, both animate and inanimate. In fact, it is in this region—Mongolia and Russian Siberia in particular—that shamanism lives on most vibrantly today.

When Koreans adopted shamanistic beliefs is unknown, but it is believed that the peoples who would eventually form the Korean nation brought shamanism with them when they migrated to the peninsula from Siberia and Manchuria in the Neolithic Era. Archaeological evidence suggests shamanism was the predominant belief system of the Korean people in prehistoric times. Korea is home to 35,000 dolmens (*goindol* in Korean), stone tombs that are believed to be indicative of a shamanistic culture. Korea's traditional foundation story, the legend of Dangun, is widely believed to be a shamanistic allegory, with the tale's transformation of bears and tigers into

(Top) An *ovoo* found at Terelj National Park, Mongolia. A shamanist cairn, an *ovoo* is similar in function to Korea's *seonangdang*. (Bottom) *Seonangdang* are cone-shaped collection of stones often found next to sacred trees at the entrance of villages or on village hills or ridges. They reveal the similarities between Mongolian and Korean folk religions.

(Left) Based on the similarity between the dress of Siberian shamans and the crowns of the kings of Silla, we can guess that Silla's rulers were "shaman-kings."

humans referring to tribes with bear and tiger totems. Similarities can be drawn with the foundation myth of the shamanistic Mongolians, who are said to have been born to a blue wolf and white deer.

Shamanism's dominance continued into Korea's Three Kingdoms Period. The early kings of Goguryeo, Baekje, and Silla could be viewed as shaman-kings of tribal peoples. This is especially evident in the beautiful golden crowns of Silla, the motifs of which betray shamanist themes and bear a strong resemblance to the headgear worn by Central Asian shamans.

The coming of Buddhism in the fourth century led to major changes in Korea's religious landscape, but shamanism remained a vital force. Rather than conflicting with the newly imported faith, shamanism enriched and complemented it. Buddhists built their temples on sacred mountains that were believed by shamans to be the home of the spirits. They even built shrines to various shamanist entities in their temples. People continued to seek the solace of shamans just as before. This coexistence continued on through the

(Middle) Painter Sin Yun-bok's 18th century painting "Mumudo," which depicts a shaminist ceremony. (Right) *Pansori*, which was designated a Masterpiece of the Oral and Intangible Heritage of Humanity by UNESCO in 2003. This traditional vocal and percussion music developed from shaman songs.

Three Kingdoms Period, the Unified Silla period (668–935), and even the Goryeo Dynasty (918–1392).

The founding of the Joseon Dynasty in 1392 and the subsequent adoption of Neo-Confucianism as Korea's ruling ideology marked the beginning of a long downturn for shamanism. Aiming to completely remake Korean society along Confucian lines, the authorities officially discouraged shamanism (as well as other faiths, most notably Buddhism). The common folk, however, continued to seek out shamans and celebrate shamanistic rituals, and the authorities could do little except turn a blind eye. Moreover, official disapproval did not extend to the arts, where shamanism continued to play a major role, particular in the fields of music and dance.

Shamanism suffered further under the Japanese, who forcibly annexed Korea as a colony in 1910. Aiming to destroy an independent Korean cultural identity, the Japanese discouraged all Korean folk religions, especially shamanism, which they worried could become a vehicle of resistance.

Renowned Korean video artist Nam June Paik performs a very unique shamanist *gut* in the 1990s. The performance blended a most Korean tradition with modern art.

Even after Korea's liberation from colonial rule in 1945, things did not immediately improve for shamanism. Not only did it have to compete with existing faiths like Buddhism and Confucianism, it now faced competition from an increasingly vibrant Protestant Christianity, which blossomed in Korea after its introduction at the turn of the 20th century. Korea's modernization-oriented elites, meanwhile, viewed shamanism as an embarrassing vestige of a past plagued by superstition and poverty. Official disapproval reached its height during the authoritarian administration of Park Chung-hee, who sought to wipe out shamanistic beliefs and practices as part of an effort to modernize rural Korean villages. To make matters worse, as society industrialized and modernized, Koreans themselves grew increasingly secular and unconcerned with the old faiths.

Shamanism's fortunes began undergoing a dramatic improvement in the 1980s. In 1987, Korea's last military dictator stepped down from power, and the country at last became a multi-party democracy. While Korea's phenomenal economic growth may have led to a general secularization of Korean society, it also inspired a greater confidence and interest in traditional culture, including shamanism. Freed from official restraints, shamanism once again blossomed.

Today, very few Koreans actually identify themselves as shamanists, but untold numbers make regular use of shamans and shamanistic rituals. In 2007, the Korea Worshipers Association, an association of shamans, estimated there were 300,000 shamans in Korea. A Reuters report from June 29, 2012, characterized the situation thusly: "Today, visiting a *mudang*—shaman priest or priestess—is so common that politicians consult them seeking answers to questions such as whether they should relocate their ancestors' remains to ensure good luck in the next election."

The *jinhongut*, a shamanist rite held to console the spirit of those who die in unexpected accidents

Basic Beliefs & Practices

Central to Korean shamanism is the role of the shaman—or *mudang*, as he or (usually) she is called in Korean—in bridging the human and spiritual worlds. It shares this with other shamanistic traditions in Siberia. The shamanist perspective posits a world

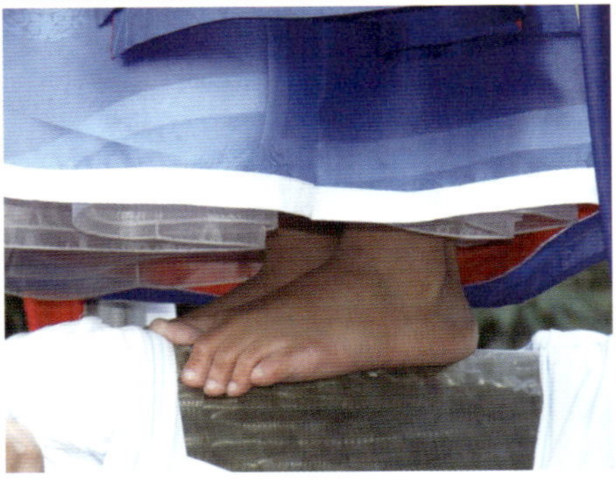

1. Images of the gods revered by *mudang*
2. A fan used in a shamanist rite 3. Jeju Yowangmajigut
4. A *gut* to console the spirits of the marines who died in the Imjin war (1592–1598): Japanese invasions of Korea
5. When possessed by the spirits, *mudang* can possess almost supernatural strength. Here, a *mudang* stands atop a razor-sharp straw cutter.

inhabited by spirits (again something it shares with shamanist traditions in Siberia). Where it differs slightly is in the fact that Korean spirits tend to inhabit heavenly bodies and geographic entities such as rocks, rivers, and mountains, whereas in Siberia the spirits are largely found in animals. Additionally, in Korea these spirits are, by and large, given human form. This leads to another difference between Korean and Siberian shamanism: when in a trance, the Siberian shaman often transforms into an animal and "travels" into the spirit world; the Korean *mudang*, on the other hand, assumes the identity of the personified spirit.

The Korean shamanist cosmology includes thousands of gods, spirits, demons, and deities. These spirits range from prominent mountains to historic generals to dead ancestors. They affect the lives and fortunes of the living in both positive and negative ways. By communicating with these spirits, the *mudang* seeks to bring good fortune to the believer—or end a string of bad fortune.

The *mudang* mediates with the spirits through the *gut*, a ritual in which offerings are made to the spirits and the *mudang* entreats them to intercede on behalf of the living. These can be ornate, colorful affairs, featuring much singing and dancing. Like shamans everywhere, the *mudang* will usually enter a trance during the *gut*. There are a wide variety of *gut*, which differ according to purpose and region; several forms are discussed in greater detail below.

Some *gut* are performed regularly at shrines, while others are requested by clients in need of help. For instance, it's not unusual for businessmen embarking on a new venture to hire a *mudang* to perform a *gut* so that the spirits will bless it. Fishing villages will hold large-scale *gut* ahead of the fishing season to pray for bountiful catches.

Many shamans also become *jeomjaengi*, or fortunetellers. *Jeomjaengi* are frequently consulted ahead of major decisions, especially the choice of a spouse.

Mudang

The *mudang* is a Korean shaman. In Korea, they are usually (although not always) women. Broadly speaking, there are two kinds: the *gangsinmu* and the *seseummu*. The biggest difference between the two is that the former are "called" to their profession, while the latter inherit their status. There are other differences as well, which we'll examine below.

Gangsinmu

Gangsinmu are *mudang* who are chosen for their role. Traditionally, they tended to be concentrated in areas of Korea north of the Hangang River. Would-be *mudang* are first afflicted by an illness known as the *sinbyeong*, or "spirit sickness." The *sinbyeong* manifests itself through poor appetite, difficulty sleeping, and hallucinations. This disease, which typically does not respond to modern medical treatment, often goes on for years, and the symptoms can get quite extreme. It is cured by a ceremony called the *naerimgut*, which not only treats the ailment but also serves as an initiation rite for the new *mudang*.

When possessed, the shaman can even swallow a sword.

Seseummu

Found largely in areas south of the Hangang River, the *seseummu* become *mudang* through inheritance—that is to say, they are born into a family of *mudang*—and learn their craft from an early age. Both the *gangsinmu* and *seseummu* perform *gut*, but while the *gangsinmu* are possessed by the spirit, the *sesummu* contact the spirits by way of a medium.

Gut

The *gut* is the most important shamanist ritual. At its core, it is a sacrifice to the spirits and an opportunity to bring together the believer and the spirits via the medium of the *mudang*. During the *gut*, the *mudang* will usually enter a trance to communicate with the spirits, or even to become one with them. The ceremonies typically feature music and dance, as well as offerings of food and drink to the spirits.

There are many forms of *gut*, differing not only according to purpose (curing disease, bringing good fortune, ferrying the dead to the next world, and so forth), but also from region to region. Still, some are more common than others. These include:

Byeolsingut

Usually led by a hereditary shaman, the *byeolsingut* is most often held in farming and fishing villages (particular on the east coast) to pray for a good catch or harvest. When held in farming villages, it is called the *pungnongje*; in fishing villages, it is called the *pungeoje*.

Hahoe Byeolsingut. In this rite, the villagers of Hahoe-ri, Andong gather at the local *seonangdang* to pray to the village's guardian spirit for health and prosperity.

Depending on the locality, it could be held yearly, or once every three, five, or ten years. It is sometimes held when new town markets are opened, too, in which case it is called a *nanjanggut*. These market rites are held every few years as a means of supporting the markets.

Dodanggut

Like the *byeolsingut*, this is a village prayer for peace and prosperity, held once every one to three years. It is most often performed in central Korea, especially in Gyeonggi-do.

Daedonggut

This rite is performed in the villages of Korea's West Sea coastal region, particularly in Hwanghae-do and the coastal region of Pyeongan-do in North Korea. It is usually held in the first, second, or third lunar month. It is a prayer for peace and prosperity

The West Sea Baeyeonsingut, a form of *daedonggut* and *pungeoje*. It's unusual in that it's performed on a boat.

invoking the protective spirits of the respective villages. In 1985, it was designated an Important Intangible Cultural Property along with the *baeyeonsingut*.

Unlike that ceremony, which is performed for individual boat owners, the *daedonggut* is a communal rite performed by villagers. It is first held in the mountains, then in each individual household in the village, and finally on the beach. Thus, the entire village becomes a stage for the rite.

Ssitgimgut

This *gut* is performed to cleanse the spirit of the deceased. It is believed that spirits cannot cross over to the next world until the bitterness of the dead has been cleansed. This is especially true when the spirit in question died before his or her time. These *gut* are most often performed along Korea's southwest coast, and on the island of Jindo in particular.

Jindo Ssitgimgut, a unique funerary rite for the benefit of both the living and the dead performed along Korea's southwest region

Two Shamanist Rituals Designated as The Intangible Cultural Heritage of Humanity by UNESCO

Chilmeoridang Yeongdeunggut

Jeju's Yeongdeunggut by the Great Shaman Kim Yun-su

To the east of Jeju City, on the slope of Sara Peak, stands Chilmeori Shrine, one of many dedicated to the various shamanic deities of Jeju Island. Chilmeori Shrine was originally located near the harbor piers, but it was moved to its present location when a new road was built. Its accessories were lost in the process, so that now only three spirit stones have been placed side by side in Sarabong Park.

To Jeju residents, who make their living from the sea, the wind is an element that controls their lives and livelihoods. Shamanist rituals are regularly held at seaside villages to pray for safety and abundance. The Yeongdeung Rites at Chilmeori Shrine (Chilmeoridang Yeongdeunggut) are a prime example of a ritual to promote the community's well-being. The ceremony was designated an Important Intangible Cultural Property by the government of Korea in 1980, and an Intangible Cultural Heritage of Humanity by UNESCO in 2009.

The ritual consists of three separate parts: a welcome rite, a farewell rite, and another rite held on Soseom (Udo), or Cow Island, where the spirit of Grandmother Yeongdeung is said to stay for one day before returning home.

1. Dapgyo Nori. This village festival, in which villagers gather to walk upon a bridge on the Danoje, is a prayer for unity and prosperity.
2. The Danoje preparations begin on the fifth day of the fourth lunar month, when the sacrificial Sinju ("Wine of the Gods") is brewed.
3. The Danoje's Daegwallyeong Guksa Seonghwang Haengcha is a rite in which the main gods—which are usually kept in shrines in the Daegwallyeong Pass—are brought into downtown Gangneung, where a *gut* and a remembrance ceremony are held.

Gangneung Danoje

Once one of Korea's most imprtant holidays, Dano (the fifth day of the fourth lunar month) is occasion for the Gangneung Danoje, a rite held in the East Coast city of Gangneung. The Dano preparations begin on the fifth day of the fourth lunar month, when the sacrificial Sinju ("Wine of the Gods") is brewed. On the 15th day of the fourth lunar month, shaman rites are held at the shrines of the Mountain God and male and female deities high up in the mountains along the Daegwallyeong Pass. A *sinmok* ("sacred tree"), a symbol of the deities, is also selected, exorcised and cut down. The tablets of the male and female dieties and the sinmok are carried down in a major procession from their mountain shrines to another shrine in the city of Gangneung itself, where more rites are held. On the third day of the fifth lunar month, the memorial tablets are carried in another procession to the Namdaecheon Stream in downtown Gangneung, where shamanist rites are held. Rites of all sorts are held over the course of the next couple of days. When the celebration is over, all the ritual objects are burned as part of a "sending off" rite to bring the spirits back to their shrines in the mountains.

Impact on Other Religions

Shamanism's interactions with Korea's other major religions have been extensive, if not always smooth.

The influence of shamanism is most readily apparent in Korean Buddhism. Buddhism was the first of the major foreign faiths to arrive on Korean shores back in the fourth century, when shamanism was Korea's dominant faith. Buddhist missionaries saw little conflict with the existing beliefs—indeed, Buddhists ultimately incorporated many of them. Buddhist temples were built on mountains regarded by the shamans as sacred. In the temples themselves, shrines were built to various shamanist deities, the most representative among them being the mountain god, or *sansin*. Virtually every Buddhist temple in Korea has a shrine to the *sansin*; even today, women who wish to conceive children often pray at these shrines. Other shamanist spirits frequently enshrined in Korean Buddhist temples include Dokseong, a hermit that appears to have originated in Buddhism but was later adopted by Korean shamans as one of their

own; and Chilseong, the seven stars of the Big Dipper (perhaps introduced to Korea via Taoism).

Shamanism's interactions with Confucianism, on the other hand, were far less fruitful. Korean Neo-Confuciansim, as practiced by the leaders of the Joseon Dynasty, was a dogmatic philosophy that sought social hegemony to the exclusion of all other competing philosophies. Accordingly, Buddhism and shamanism were officially discouraged, if not outright suppressed. In the countryside, shamanist rituals and beliefs were tolerated, but in polite society Confucian ethics and norms were to be followed.

Korean Christianity, too, initially took a dim view of shamanism. Early Western missionaries were openly contemptuous of shamanist beliefs, and these attitudes were passed on to their Korean students. Still, even Christianity could not avoid being influenced. In particular, the prevalence of charismatic prayer and preaching in Korean Protestant churches is often explained as a product of Korea's shamanist heritage.

Mokgye Byeolshinje. This is a remembrance ceremony held in villages in Chungju in which villagers pray to their villages' protective gods for the safety of boatman and the villages themselves. It combines a shamanist *gut* and the Confucian remembrance ceremony.

Shaman Kim Kum-hwa

"May a shaman be born to your household!"

This is what a shaman says when she's really angry, it shows how cruel life can be for a *mudang*. When Kim Kum-hwa, 81, acknowledged leader of northern-style ecstatic shamanism and "living national treasure," dances atop the razor-sharp blades of a double-edged knife during a *gut*, she wields the power of the ancient generals, but things are a lot different when she steps back to earth.

Of Korea's many shamans, Kim may be the best known, especially internationally, a fact in no small part attributable to her many performances overseas. Initiated as a shaman at the age of 17, she has not only devoted her life to her craft, but also made tireless efforts to boost the profile of shamanism within Korea and shatter modern-day prejudices about her beliefs.

"Over the years, I've suffered a great deal. I've lost loved ones and money. Until recently, I felt as if I'd spent my life all alone hanging off the edge of a cliff. Only now, as my life is drawing to a close, have I been able to walk on stable ground."

Perhaps this is why Kim cries each time she officiates at a *naerimgut*, the initiation ceremony in which a spirit takes over the body of a shaman. It breaks her heart to think of the hardships the newly initiated shaman will go through in his or her lifetime.

YI: How many times have you performed the *naerimgut*? Did all the new initiates go on to become shamans?

KIM: I've performed more than 20 *naerimgut*. I've established a master-disciple relationship with each one of the new initiates, but they haven't all become shamans, and I wouldn't want them to. In my view, the purpose of the *naerimgut* is to treat people suffering from *sinbyeong* (the mystical sickness caused by the descent of a spirit or a god) and help them recover their health and lead a happy family life. Why should they all become shamans? When I perform a *naerimgut*, I make a clear distinction between those I plan to cultivate as disciples and those I simply want to treat and return to a normal life.

The Great shaman Kim Kum-hwa performs the West Sea Baeyeonsingut during the closing ceremony of the 2009 Korea—Japan Hanmadang Festival in Tokyo.

Jakdu geori

YI: The Hwanghae *naerimgut* is especially famous for the *bisu geori* (a *geori* refers to an individual section of a shamanistic rite), a unique form of the *jakdu geori* in which a knife-riding general enters the body of the shaman and dances with the double-edged chopper. Can you give us a brief explanation of this portion of the *gut*?

KIM: The altar consists of a seven-layered tower constructed from a steel drum, wooden dough boards, a small table, a pine board, a water pitcher, and a brass bowl with the *jakdu*, a double-edged knife, on the very top. The shaman presses the razor-sharp blades of the knife against her arms and legs and her tongue and inside her cheeks. There aren't any cuts, just impressions where the blades have been pressed against her skin. Then she climbs up onto the blades and dances. It's at that point that she delivers the gods' messages to the audience. The apprentice shamans do exactly as the head shaman does.

YI: It is said that the shaman embodies the spirit of military generals, such as Choi Yeong (1316–1388, one of the great generals of the Goryeo Dynasty), Yi Sun-sin (1545–1598, a Joseon Dynasty period's admiral who fought the Japanese invaders) or Im Kyong-om (1594–1646, another oseon Dynasty period's admiral who fought the Manchus), when she is up on the knife blades. Why is that? Why not the spirit of a king?

KIM: The king ruled the state, but his servants, the generals, were the ones who wielded the actual power. For example, Choi Yeong fought gallantly for his kingdom and country, but ultimately died an unjust death. When a shaman is up on those blades, she wields the power of the great generals against all misfortune and evil spirits.

YI: It was hard to watch the shaman run those blades across her arms and press them against her tongue. I know this is a dumb question, but have you ever tried that when you weren't performing a *gut*?

KIM: You can't do it at any other time.

YI: Experienced tight rope walkers say the rope actually looks quite wide after they've trained for a long time. What about the knife blades? Do they look sharp during a *gut*?

KIM: Of course. They'll slice a cucumber or pear in half at the drop of a hat. The gods make sure the blades are sharp.

YI: Aren't you afraid?

KIM: After dancing around for a while, I can't tell if it's me moving or the blades themselves. I'm not conscious of what I'm doing. There are times when I'm afraid, usually when I'm ill at ease or frustrated.

YI: The *gut* is relatively small in scale compared to Christian or Buddhist services. As a result, the sense of wonder or the miracles experienced during the *gut* doesn't seem to last long. Considering shamanism's relative lack of evangelical strength, what do you see as the future of the belief in Korea?

KIM: Actually, I'm concerned about that. The government has no policy on preserving *gut*. Thankfully, they've designated it an Important Intangible Cultural Property now. The various Christian organizations are wrong to protest the inclusion of *gut* in overseas cultural tours, which already include masked dance and *pansori*. We haven't ever objected to Christian or Buddhist events, have we? Actually, those religions aren't even indigenous to Korea, so why are they making such a big deal about shamanism, a religion rooted in Korea's own culture? I hope that *gut* will be recognized as an art form.

YI: However, if we look at *gut* as a religion, rather than an art form, it is clear that people actually fear it. It seems this is the reason behind the difficulties you've had propagating the belief.

KIM: There's nothing to be afraid of. Shamanism was the religion of our grandparents long before these other religions were introduced from abroad. By believing in shamanism, we can unite as one, and isn't that the road to the unification in Korea?

2 Chapter Two

BUDDHISM

Since its arrival in Korea in the second half of the fourth century, Buddhism has had a tremendous impact on Korea's spiritual and cultural landscape. For most of the Three Kingdoms Period, and all of the Unified Silla and Goguryeo dynasties, Buddhism was not only the dominant religion in Korea, but also the religion of state. Buddhism lost its dominant position in Korean society with the rise of the Confucian Joseon Dynasty at the end of the 14th century, but the religion continued to inspire the faithful, especially in the countryside, where great monasteries dotted the mountainsides. The artistic, architectural, musical and literary heritage the faith has given Korea cannot be overstated.

Today, roughly 22% of Koreans identify themselves as Buddhists, making it Korea's second largest religion behind Christianity. Once endangered in its own homeland, Korean Buddhism is now a vital force both in Korea and overseas, where Korean missionaries are bringing the dharma to an international audience.

History

Buddhism originated in India some 2,400 years ago and came to the Korean Peninsula via China in the fourth century. It first arrived in the Korean kingdoms of Goguryeo and Baekje in 372 and 384, respectively. The new faith was warmly received in both kingdoms. Its reception was considerably colder in Silla, where it first entered in the fifth century. According to the *Samguk Yusa*, a 13th century Korean history text, the turning point took place in 527, when a Buddhist court official by the name of Ichadon was martyred. (Legend holds that when he was beheaded, milk poured from his neck instead of blood.) Under King Chinhung (r. 540–576), Buddhism was made the state religion of Silla.

When Silla unified Korea in 668, the peninsula experienced a

Templestay at Golgulsa Temple. Golgulsa is famous for its martial art of Seonmudo, traditionally used by the monks as a form of meditation.

golden age of peace and stability. Buddhism flourished under state patronage. Countless temples were built throughout the country, including Gyeongju's grand Bulguksa Temple. Several of Korea's greatest Buddhist theologians—among them the great monks Wonhyo and Uisang—were active during this period, too. Toward the end of Silla, the practice of Seon—better known in the West as "Zen"—began to take root.

Buddhism continued to flourish under the Goryeo Dynasty (918–1392), where Buddhism was the state religion. During this period, there was a movement toward reconciling scholastic Buddhism—with its emphasis on learning the Buddhist sutras—and Zen, which emphasized enlightenment through meditation.

Unfortunately, state patronage also led to corruption, and by the end of the Goryeo period Confucian scholars were attacking the vice and greed of the Buddhist temples, which often controlled considerable land and wealth. When Confucians took control of the country and established the Joseon kingdom (1392–1910), they placed stringent new conditions on Buddhism. They limited the

(Left) Site of Hwangnyongsa Temple, the most spectacular of the Silla capital of Gyeongju. The temple was burned down by the Mongols in 1238. (Middle) Mock-up of Hwangryongsa Temple during Silla dynasty, Gyeongju (Right) Samyeong Daesa (1544–1610), who gathered an army of Buddhist monks to defend Korea during the Japanese invasions of the late 16th century number of temples, restricted who could join the monkhood, and, most notably, drove the temples into the mountains. Buddhist monks were barred from the cities. The situation began to improve somewhat in the 16th century, however, thanks to the active participation of Buddhist monks as warriors in the Imjin War (1592–1598) against the Japanese.

In modern times, Buddhism has had to hold its own against the rising popularity of Christianity and a general trend toward secularism and materialism resulting from Korea's industrialization and modernization. Overall, it hasn't done too poorly—nearly half of Koreans who consider themselves religious are Buddhists. Moreover, even non-Buddhists generally recognize the rich heritage that the religion has left Korea.

Like Christianity, Korean Buddhism is broken into several sects, the most prominent being the Jogye Order, which merges *gyo* (scholastic Buddhism) and Seon (Zen).In keeping with Korean tradition, its monks are celibate. The order controls most of Korea's major Buddhist temples, including its headquarters, Jogyesa,which is located in downtown Seoul.

Basic Beliefs

Like Buddhists throughout the world, Korean Buddhists follow the teachings of Siddhartha Gautama. Better known as the Buddha, he was an Indian prince who gave up his royal calling to become a spiritual teacher in the fifth century BC. The Buddha's teachings focus primarily on the nature of suffering and its alleviation through achieving a state of enlightenment, or nirvana. Indeed, it's from this state of enlightenment that the Buddha took his name—a Sanskrit word that means "awakened one." His teachings are contained in a large number of texts, called sutras, which have been assembled into a

Wonhyo & Uisang

Wonhyo

Uisang

Silla was a period of great intellectual development for Korean Buddhism. This is best exemplified by the lives of the era's two greatest monks, Wonhyo and Uisang.

Close personal friends, they took very different religious paths. According to tradition, their point of divergence came as they were making their way to China to further their studies. Just prior to embarking on the sea voyage to China, the two spent the night in a cave, taking refuge from a torrential downpour. Thirsty, Wonhyo fumbled around in the darkness and found what he thought was a gourd full of refreshing water. He took a long drink and went back to sleep, satiated. When the two awoke the next morning, they learned the cave was actually a tomb, and the gourd was actually a human skull full of dirty water. For Wonhyo, this was an enlightening experience—he was amazed at the mind's ability to transform the disgusting into a pleasant experience. Satisfied, he abandoned his voyage to China and bid his friend farewell.

Wonhyo was a prolific writer—he wrote about 80 commentaries, many of which were incredibly influential not only in Korea, but also in China and Japan. His genius lay in the way he

Oeosa Temple in Pohang, where the great Silla monks Wonhyo and Uisang studied

managed to find the essential underlying truth in Silla's many schools of thought. His synthetic view of Buddhism had a tremendous impact on Korea's religious worldview, specifically with its tendency towards syncretism. He eventually abandoned the clergy altogether and became a layman, dedicating his life to teaching the masses through song and dance. He even married a Silla princess, who gave birth to a son who eventually became one of the kingdom's greatest Confucian scholars.

Uisang, on the other hand, went to China, where he became a student of Zhiyan, the patriarch of the Avatamsaka School (Huayan in Chinese, Hwaeom in Korean) of Mahayana Buddhism. He took the Avatamsaka philosophy back with him to Korea, where he made it the dominant school of Silla. Founded in the *Avatamsaka Sutra*, the philosophy is based on the belief that "all are one." In addition to his scholastic work, Uisang is known as a prolific temple builder, founding many of Korea's most important Buddhist monasteries.

Palman Daejanggyeong

The Temple of Haeinsa, on Mount Gaya, is home to the Tripitaka Koreana , the most complete collection of Buddhist texts, engraved on 80,000 woodblocks between 1237 and 1248. The buildings of Janggyeong Panjeon, which date from the 15th century, were constructed to house the woodblocks, which are also revered as exceptional works of art. As the oldest depository of the Tripitaka , they reveal an astonishing mastery of the invention and implementation of the conservation techniques used to preserve these woodblocks.

- Inscription, UNESCO

The Palman Daejanggyeong ("Eighty Thousand Tripitaka")—better known in the West as the *Tripitaka Koreana*—is the world's most complete collection of the Buddhist canon in Chinese characters. The original was carved in the late 11th century, but was lost in 1232 during the Mongol invasion of the Goryeo Dynasty. To evade the notoriously water-shy invaders, the court relocated to the island of Ganghwado, where it ordered another copy carved as a plea for divine assistance in repelling the invaders.

The project took 16 years, and while it did little against the Mongols, it did produce one of the crown jewels of East Asian Buddhist culture.

The Palman Daejanggyeong

The entire Mahayana Buddhist canon was carved into 81,258 wooden blocks, organized into 1,496 titles and 6,568 volumes. All told, the collection consists of 52,382,960 Chinese characters, without a single error. Each block measures 70 cm by 24 cm and contains 23 lines of text with 14 characters per line. Thirty monks are

Haeinsa Temple's Janggyeongpanjeon,
where the Palman Daejanggyeong is stored and preserved

believed to have participated in the project.

The woodblocks were carved out of the finest birch wood from the islands off southern Korea. Pieces were soaked in seawater for two years, cut, and boiled in salt water. They were then exposed to the wind and elements for three years, carved, and covered in poisonous lacquer to keep pests away.

In 1398, the collection was moved to its current home at Haeinsa Temple at the foot of Mt. Gayasan in southeast Korea. Two massive wooden repositories were erected in the 15th century to house it. These are marvels in and of themselves—built expressly to preserve the woodblock collection, they use nature and architecture to regulate humidity and create an ideal preservation environment. The location prevents damp winds from entering from the south and cold winds from entering from the north. The repositories' slatted windows—sized differently in the north and south halls—keep the halls well ventilated, and the materials absorb excess humidity in the summer and retain it in the winter.

The Palman Daejanggyeong has enjoyed much good fortune. The halls survived the late 16th century Japanese invasions of Korea, when many other temples were burnt to the ground. During the Korean War, a South Korean pilot disobeyed orderes to bomb the temple, which had been taken over by the communists. In 1995, the woodblock prints and the hall in which they are kept were added to UNESCO's list of World Heritage Sites.

canon. Korea, in fact, is home to an especially spectacular example of one: the *Tripitaka Koreana*, a complete woodblock edition of the canon that was carved in the 13th century.

Korean Buddhism belongs to the Mahayana tradition, the larger of the two major Buddhist traditions. The predominant tradition in China, Korea, and Japan, it emphasizes seeking enlightenment to help all sentient beings, whereas the other major tradition, Theravada (predominant in Sri Lanka and Southeast Asia), emphasizes individual enlightenment through monastic life.

Buddhism teaches several doctrines. The first is the "Four Noble Truths." These truths are 1) life is suffering, 2) the cause of suffering is desire, 3) we can end suffering by ending desire, 4) to end desire we should follow the "Eightfold Path" of 1) right view, 2) right intention, 3) right speech, 4) right action, 5) right livelihood, 6) right effort, 7) right mindfulness, and 8) right concentration. The emphasis is on practice rather than belief.

In Korea, there is a distinction between the Buddhist laity and the monastic clergy. Korea's monks and nuns—who are traditionally celibate, although some smaller Korean Buddhist orders allow their clergy to marry—largely reside in temples, monasteries, and hermitages. Temples are almost always located in mountain areas, where the scenery and quiet are conducive to concentration.

Seon vs. Gyo

Korean Buddhists employ a number of methods to achieve enlightenment. Perhaps most typical—and most commonly studied overseas—is Seon, better known in the West by its Japanese name Zen. This school of Buddhist practice, which came to Korea through China in the late Unified Silla period, centers on meditation—seated meditation in particular—as a direct means of achieving enlightenment. A common meditation tool in Korea is the *hwadu*, in which the practitioner meditates on a specific, often seemingly unanswerable, question. These questions cannot be answered using logic; they can only be answered through meditation.

Seon is generally practiced by monks in monasteries, although laypeople—and even non-Buddhists—can and do practice it as well. Seon is almost always studied under respected masters, who themselves form a lineage over the generations.

Another school of Buddhist practice is *gyo*, which could be described as scholastic Buddhism. *Gyo* students seek knowledge and wisdom in Buddhism's sacred texts, or sutras. In the case of the Jogye Order of Korean Buddhism, the country's dominant Buddhist sect, particular attention is placed on the *Diamond Sutra*, a treatise on illusion and impermanence. Also influential, particularly historically, has been the *Lotus Sutra*, which emphasizes devotion and faith in achieving enlightenment.

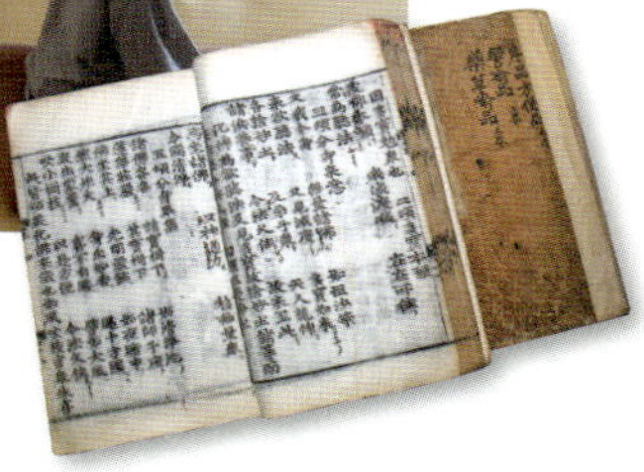

(Top) Monks practicing sitting meditation during the summer retreat (Bottom) The *Lotus Sutra*. With its emphasis that all the Buddha's teachings led to one enlightenment, the sutra has been an important underpinning of Korea's religious harmony and tolerance.

Kwan Um School of Zen

Memorial ceremony marking the third year after the passing of Zen Master Seung Sahn

Korean Seon (Zen) practice is getting an increasingly warm reception from overseas audiences. Korean Seon centers can be found in cities in around the world, while about 400 foreign monks were active in Korea as of the end of 2011. In May 2012, a Jogye Order study session for foreign monks was attended by about 60 monks.

Playing a key role in the globalization of Korean Buddhism is the Kwan Um School of Zen, described by one American Zen Buddhist priest as the largest school of Zen in the Western world. It was founded in 1983 by Zen Master SeungSahn. Born in 1927 to Presbyterian parents in northern Korea, Seung Sahn was studying Western philosophy at university when a monk friend of his lent him a copy of the *Diamond Sutra*. Inspired, he left school to become a monk in 1948. In 1972, he moved to the United States and took up work as a laundromat repairman in Providence, Rhode Island. He soon gained students from nearby Brown University, before long, he was founding Zen centers in cities throughout the United States, including Los Angeles, New York, and Providence. This was just the beginning—there are currently over 100 Kwan Um Zen centers in 27 countries, with the United States and Eastern Europe especially well represented.

Seung Sahn passed away in 2004, but his international community is still going strong. In Korea, the Kwan Um School maintains a number of Zen centers, including its regional headquarters at Musangsa Temple (near

Daejeon) and Seoul Zen Center at Hwagyesa Temple in northern Seoul. Life at these centers is very much like life at any Korean Buddhist temple—the days are filled with chanting, bowing, and, of course, Seon meditation. In accordance with Korean Seon practice, intensive three-month retreats are conducted in the summer and winter. During these retreats, monks and nuns engage in intensive sitting meditation. Talking is kept to an absolute minimum.

Dae Bong Sunim

Dae Bong Sunim is a head monk of Musangsa Temple and in many ways typical of the foreign-born monks, albeit with a past a tad more colorful. Born Larry Sichel in Philadelphia in 1950, he worked as an orderly in psychiatric hospitals in Connecticut and a welder in a shipyard building nuclear submarines. All the while, he sought answers on suffering and the end of suffering. After exploring New England's Zen centers, he attended a 1977 lecture where he met Korean Zen Master Seung Sahn. He was so impressed that he quit his job at the shipyard and moved into Providence Zen Center, where he spent seven years as a layperson before becoming an ordained Buddhist monk.

Dae Bong Sunim explains that life as a monk and life as a layperson are not all that different. "The monk life and the layperson life are not really different," he says. "Situations are different sometimes, but the basic issues are my own desire, anger, and ignorance, and I can see through them to the root and let them go. Then some wisdom appears, and you begin to know how to deal with situations that appear in a way that benefits you and the other person, that benefits everybody. Then you are making spiritual progress."

The two schools are not mutually exclusive—while monks tend to specialize in one or the other, Seon monks will study the sutras and *gyo* monks will practice Seon. The Jogye Order was in fact founded by a Zen master, Bojo Jinul, who wanted to bring the two schools together under one roof.

Buddhist Monks and Nuns

Korean Buddhism is monastic—that is to say, members of its clergy renounce their worldly existence to dedicate their lives to religious practice.

Those who wish to become a monk must first find a teacher at a Buddhist temple. The aspirant will cut his or her hair short and undergo an apprenticeship that usually lasts about five months.

Upon the completion of their winter retreat, monks spend about three months traveling the country to ensure their study went well.

In order to become a true monk, trainees must undergo an initiation ceremony.

After this, the aspirant takes the novice precepts and undergoes a four-year training period at a monastery or other training center, learning the ins and outs of Buddhist philosophy and practice. After this, he or she will take a test. If the novice passes, he or she takes the full precepts and becomes a monk or nun.

Monks and nuns live very simple, ascetic lives. They wake up before sunrise and go to bed early. Their daily routine is characterized by chanting, meditation, simple meals, and temple chores. Typically, Korean monks and nuns wear simple gray robes. In accordance with Buddhist principles, Buddhist meals are vegetarian. The monks and nuns of Korea's largest Buddhist sect, the Jogye Order of Korean Buddhism, are celibate; some smaller orders allow their monks and nuns to marry.

Korean Buddhist Temples

The main religious sanctuary of Korean Buddhism is the temple. You'd be hard-pressed to find a prominent mountain in Korea without a Buddhist temple on it. Temples come in all sizes, from small hilltop hermitages to grand monasteries. Many of Korea's

temples have histories that stretch back over a millennium, and are home to rich collections of artistic and architectural treasures.

Most Buddhist temples are located on scenic mountains far from the hustle and bustle of the city. Typically, temples—especially the larger ones—are entered through a series of gates, including the Iljumun ("one pillar gate"), which marks the entrance of the compound; and the Sacheonwangmun ("gate of the Celestial Guardians of the Four Directions"), which contains images or statues of the temple's spiritual guardians.

The precinct itself is usually composed of several halls arranged into several courtyards. The main courtyard is where you'll find the main Buddha hall, which is usually where the largest Buddha image is housed. This is also where laypeople conduct most of their devotions, and hence is frequently the busiest hall in the temple. You will also find many other halls dedicated to various incarnations of the Buddha or Buddhist concepts. The monks' living

A view of Yeongju's Buseoksa Temple

quarters—and their meditation hall—are typically placed off to the side, separate from the main complex. Visitors are usually banned from entering this area.

Pagodas can often be seen at Buddhist temples, especially in the main courtyard. Modeled on the stupas found in India, these towers contain the relics of great monks and other religious artifacts. They almost always have an odd number of tiers as odd numbers are considered auspicious in yin-yang theory. Korean pagodas are almost always made of stone, unlike pagodas in Japan (where they are made of wood) and China (brick). Korean stone masons have shown particular skill over the centuries, so in addition to beautiful pagodas, you'll often find other lovely pieces of stonework, too, including lanterns, bridges, and terraces.

Larger Buddhist temples often have one or more hermitages, usually located some distance away further up the mountain. These hermitages provide an even quieter place for monks to practice.

Map of Songgwangsa, One of the "Three Jewels" of Korean Buddhism

1 Iljumun ("one pillar gate"),
2 Uhwagak ("a bridge of enlightenment")
3 Sacheonwangmun ("a gate of the Celestial Guardians of the Four Directions")
4 Jongnugak ("a bell tower")
5 Daeungbojeon ("the main Buddha hall")
6 Jijangjeon ("a hall for Ksitigarbha, Earth Treasury")

A pagoda of
the great monk Uisang

Buddhist Art

Buddhism has bequeathed a rich artistic heritage to Korea. Of its roughly 230 National Treasures, about half are connected to Buddhism. Visit any Buddhist temple and you'll be treated to a gorgeous array of Buddhist architecture, paintings, and statuary.

Statues

Almost all Buddhist temples have a main Buddha statue, usually housed in the main Buddha hall. Often, the statue will represent Sakyamuni, or the historical Buddha, but other manifestations of the Buddha may be represented, too. Bodhisattva (enlightened beings who seek the enlightenment of all sentient beings, and are thus a model of Mahayana Buddhism) are frequently depicted in statue form. One commonly shown bodhisattva is the Avalokiteśvara, or bodhisattva of compassion, who, unlike most other Buddhas and bodhisattvas, is usually presented as a woman.

Most Korean Buddhist states are made of gilt bronze, but some—especially older ones—may be made from wood or cast iron. Some of the images can be quite large: the ones in the main Buddha hall of Seoul's Jogyesa Temple, for instance, are about 520 cm high.

Murals & Paintings

Buddhist temples are full of paintings, beginning with the temple halls themselves. These are colorfully painted with a traditional red and green color scheme that is not only decorative, but also preserves the wood. Halls frequently sport colorful and instructive murals, too, conveying Buddhist tales and legends or serving as tools to teach Buddhist precepts and practice. These murals can be found either inside or outside the halls. One series of murals you are likely to find is the Ten Oxherding Pictures, which represent the 10 stages of becoming a bodhisattva.

1

2

3

4

5

1. Pensive Bodhisattva from the sixth century and Gilt-Bronze Pensive Maitreya Bodhisattva from the later Three Kingdoms period
2. Wall murals of Woljeongsa Temple, Pyeongchang
3. Interior of Gyeongju's Seokguram Grotto, the best example of Korean Buddhist grotto architecture of the Unified Silla period. Registered as a UNESCO World Heritage Site.
4. 13th century "Water Moon Avalokitesvara" painting from the Goryeo Dynasty
5. Dancheong painting of Tongdosa Temple in Yangsan

Music and Dance

Buddhist temples are not, by and large, musical places, although there are plenty of beautiful sounds to be heard, including chanting, the temple bell, and the wooden gong. One especially important musical tradition is the Yeongsanjae, a grand musical reenactment of the Buddha's delivery of the *Lotus Sutra*. This is performed 49 days after the death of a believer, and aims to help both the deceased and the living attain enlightenment. The rite is accompanied by music, dance, and chanting, and has been listed as a UNESCO Intangible Treasure.

The Yeongsanjae, a Buddhist rite to convey the soul of the dead on his or her 49th day of passing. Initially a recreation of the Buddha's sermon to his disciples atop Vulture Peak, the rite transformed into a prayer so that the dead may enter Nirvana after it came to Korea during the Silla period.

Temple Stay

The Temple Stay program began as an experimental program during the 2002 Korea-Japan World Cup. Today, a decade later, it has blossomed into one of Korea's best-loved cultural tourism programs. Some 42 temples around Korea—most in scenic mountain locations far from the hustle and bustle of urban Korea—host two-day programs where visitors of all faiths and nationalities can get in touch with nature—and themselves—and experience a 1,700-year-old tradition.

Let us take a look at a typical Templestay program at one of Korea's most beautiful Buddhist monasteries, Gongju's Magoksa Temple.

Mountain and Temple

Hidden in the mountains a few kilometers to the north of the west-central town of Gongju, Magoksa Temple has a relatively isolated location, ensuring its relative tranquility compared to other temples its size. The complex itself is a treasure trove of Korean architecture, home to several National Treasures. The temple is surrounded by thick, fragrant forests and rushing rivers, which provide space for reflection and renewal.

A Two-Day at Temple amidst Pine and Wind

Magoksa hosts a two-day *sansa* ("mountain and temple") program on Saturday and Sunday (along with tailored programs during the week). It starts at 2pm with instruction in basic temple etiquette and, most importantly in how to bow. These lessons are followed by a tour of the temple and an hour's *pohaeng* (walking meditation) amidst the surrounding hills and forests.

Afterwards, you head to the cafeteria for *gongyang*, or Buddhist meals. In accordance with Buddhist tradition, meals are vegetarian; signs posted in the room remind visitors, "Eating is practice, too." Like the monks, you wash your own dishes after you're done—as much a part of practice as Seon meditation itself.

After dinner, there is evening chanting in Magoksa's main hall, followed by an hour's meditation in a hall set off to the side of the complex. For many, this is one of the highlights of the program, although it's by no means easy. Once you've given your mind a workout, it's time to give the rest of you a workout with the 108 bows. By the time you're finished with this, it's 9 pm, and you're ready for bed. It will be one of the best sleeps you've had, but it won't last long.

The next day, it's up at 4 am. By 4:30, you're gathering in the main hall for the morning chanting. At 5 am—just as the sun is rising—it's another 108 bows. The second day is relatively relaxing—talks with the monks, a morning *gongyang*, some communal chores, photo-taking, and other activities before lunch and departure. Hopefully, you'll leave with greater awareness than when you went in.

Gongyang

The formal meals taken at Buddhist temples. Entirely vegetarian, they are simple and nutritious. You are supposed to eat only in moderation, wasting not a single grain or leaf. After you are finished, be sure to wash the bowls yourself.

108 Bows

Through the 108 bows the prostrations, in which you repent by lowering your body completely, you can cleanse yourself of the sufferings you accumulate through your actions.

Meditation

Meditation comes in all forms. Formal seated meditation—called *jwaseon* in Korean—may be the most typical, but in truth everything you do should be a form of practice.

Yebul

Formal chanting, usually before the main Buddha image of the temple. Typically, this involves chanting the "Homage to the Buddha" and the *Heart Sutra*.

MORE INFO

Cost: 60,000 won for weekend stay
Registration: Visit www.magoksa.co.kr (Korean) or call (041) 841-6226
Time: Please arrive before 2 pm Saturday.
Getting There: Buses to Gongju depart from Seoul's Express Bus Terminal (travel time: 1 hr, 50 min). From Gongju, transfer to a bus to Magoksa (travel time: 40 min).

3

Chapter Three

CONFUCIANISM

Korea has often called the world's most Confucian nation. For the five centuries of the Joseon Dynasty, Confucianism was its ruling ideology; the dynasty's rulers attempted, and to a great extent succeeded, in transforming what had been a largely Buddhist nation into the model of a Confucian civilization. Even in the modern, consumer-driven culture of 21st century Korea, Confucian ethics and practices are still very much alive, influencing virtually every aspect of society, including family life, public behavior, the workplace, and the classroom.

Confucianism is not a religion per se—it's an ethical and philosophical system that aims to develop personal virtue and promote social and political harmony. Very, very few Koreans identify themselves as "Confucianists," as such, but almost all Koreans—regardless of professed faith—follow its norms, especially in public life. Confucian ideals and aesthetics have left a lasting impact on Korea's traditional art and music, too.

History

Confucianism (*yugyo* in Korean) is a system of ethics and philosophy based on the moral, religious, and political teachings of the Chinese philosopher Kǒngzǐ (551 BC–479 BC)—better known in the West by his Latinized name, Confucius. At its heart, it is a highly humanistic system that seeks to instill benevolence through the development of personal character. Humans develop character through study, self-improvement, ritual, and community life. Great emphasis is placed on learning, interpersonal relationships, respect for your elders, tradition, and relations between rulers and the ruled. For Confucianists, the ideal man was part scholar, part saint.

Confucianism has been part of the Korean cultural landscape since at least as far back as the Three Kingdoms Period, when Chinese political and educational systems were adopted by Korean

The Seokjeon Daeje at Seoul's Munmyo Shrine on Sungkyunkwan. The rite, held in the spring and fall, honors Confucius and renowned Chinese and Korean Confucian scholars.

polities. It got an extra boost in the Goryeo Dynasty when King Gwangjong (r. 949–975) instituted the Confucian civil service exam—the *gwageo*—which tested participants' knowledge of classical Chinese texts as a prerequisite for political office. Still, throughout the Three Kingdoms, Unified Silla, and Goryeo periods, Confucianism's impact was limited largely to the administrative sphere, while the state religion of Buddhism had a much greater impact on culture and society.

This all changed at the end of the 14th century. As the Goryeo Dynasty decayed, Korea's Confucian scholars grew increasingly vocal. In 1392, General Yi Seong-gye launched a coup and, with the support of Confucian officials, founded the Joseon Dynasty, which would rule Korea for the next 500 years. Joseon's new rulers favored a school of thought known as Neo-Confucianism, a form of Confucianism that borrowed spiritual and metaphysical elements of Taoism and Buddhism; its most famous advocate was the 12th century Song Dynasty scholar Zhu Xi.

Under its neo-Confucian elites, the new dynasty revolutionized Korea—Buddhism was jettisoned, and all aspects of society were reorganized along Confucian lines. Joseon was ruled absolutely by a king assisted by a court of scholar-officials

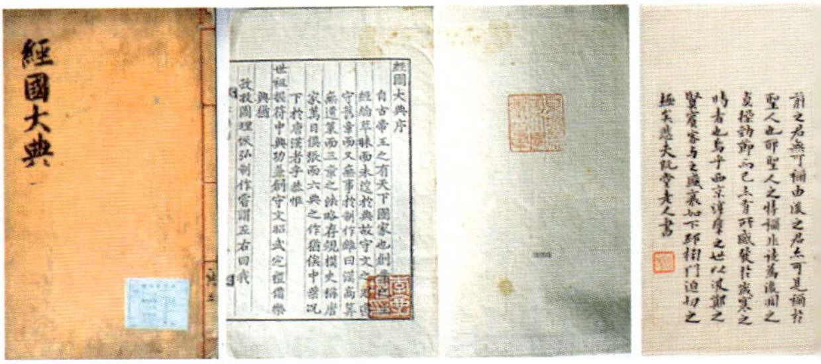

schooled in Confucian learning. At the top of the social ladder was a scholar-elite class known as the *yangban*, who (at least in theory) owed their position to their mastery of the Confucian classics. Below them, society was further divided into middle and lower classes. Great emphasis was placed on rites and ceremonies, especially those intended to honor ancestors. In the arts, the more ostentatiously ornate designs favored by previous dynasties were abandoned in favor of simpler, more rustic motifs.

Korean Confucianism underwent a Golden Age in the 16th century with the appearance of its two greatest scholars, Yi Hwang (1501–1570, also known as "Toegye") and Yi I (1536–1584, also

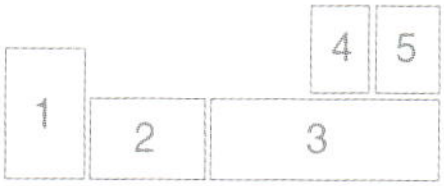

1. Confucius 2. The *Gyeonggukdaejeon*, which formed the basis of Confucian rule during the Joseon Dynasty
3. "Winter Landscape in Winter" (1844). Painted by late Joseon Dynasty scholar Kim Jeong-hui, the painting is a wonderful example of *muninhwa*, paintings produced by *seonbi* rather than professional painters.
4. Yi I, a great Confucian scholar in Joseon Dynasty 5. Yi Hwang, a great Confucian scholar in Joseon Dynasty

Jeong Yak-yong and Silhak

Scholar, official, and philosopher Jeong Yak-yong (1762–1836) is regarded by many as the greatest thinker of the later Joseon Dynasty. Better known by his pen name of Dasan ("Tea Mountain"), he strove to incorporate modern ideas into Joseon's dominant Neo-Confucian ideology and make it more relevant to contemporary life. His efforts were not always appreciated by conservative officials, however, and he spent much of his life in exile.

Jeong was born in what is now Namyangju, Gyeonggi-do, as the youngest of four brothers. While distinguished, his family was also poor, having supported the wrong side in one of the interminable factional struggles of the late Joseon Dynasty royal court. Still, the brothers showed considerable academic talent, and when visionary, reform-minded King Jeongjo came to power in 1776, their stars began to rise.

Jeong was an adherent of *silhak*, or "Practical Learning." This movement, which began in the 17th century, was aimed at reinterpreting Neo-Confucianism to address contemporary problems. This involved adopting new technologies and ideas—some from the West via China, where Jesuit missionaries had been employed at the Ming court since the 16th century. It also involved refocusing Confucianism on real-world problems such as poverty and defense, rather than semantic debates. Jeong's embrace of new ideas, and his concern for worldly issues, can be seen most dramatically at Suwon's Hwaseong Fortress, the

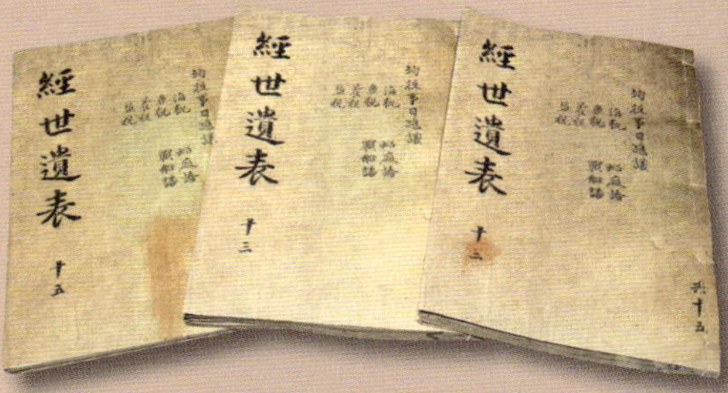

The *Gyeongseyupo* (1816). Written during Jeong's exile in Gangjin, the book called for systemic reforms, including reforms to administrative bodies and the tax and land systems.

construction of which he oversaw. Today designated a UNESCO World Heritage Site, it was built with modern construction techniques—including pulleys and cranes—and according to sound strategic principles.

Among the new ideas that entered Korea was Roman Catholicism, and the Jeong brothers were among the very first converts. King Jeongjo tacitly tolerated Catholics, but the situation changed drastically after he died. Queen Regent Jeongsun was a factional foe of reformers like Jeong, and she launched a bloody purge of her enemies, citing the "perverse" new faith as a reason.

Jeong was exiled to Gangjin, where he spent 18 years residing in a small thatched-roof cottage. There he taught local students, chatted with the monks of nearby Baengnyeonsa Temple, and wrote, penning about 500 works during the exile, including two of his masterpieces: one tract on local governance, and another on land reform and strengthening the economy and national defense. In 1819, King Sunjo, now in his majority, pardoned Jeong and allowed him to return to his hometown, where he maintained a low profile until his death in 1836 .

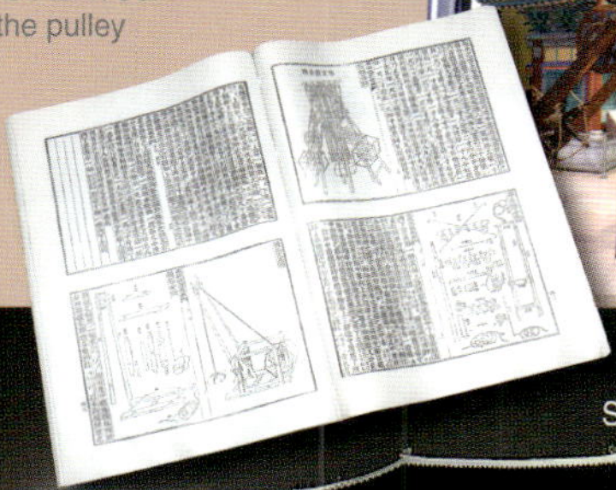

(Left) Records from the construction of Suwon Fortress from 1794 to 1796. (Right) The Geojunggi, the pulley system designed by Jeong Yak-yong. With just a little energy, a person could lift very heavy objects.

Janganmun Gate, the front entrance of Suwon Hwaseong Fortress

Young students respectfully greeting their teacher at a *seodang*, a private Confucian academy

known as "Yulgok"). A second Golden Age came in the 17th and 18th centuries with the Silhak movement, a school of Confucian thought that emphasized science and practical knowledge.

Confucianism's role as a ruling ideology ended with the collapse of the Joseon Dynasty in 1910. Today, very few Koreans would identify themselves as a Confucianist, but Confucianism's impact on Korean culture and society is still very evident. Koreans' famous thirst for education is a Confucian legacy, as is the culture of test-taking in Korean schools. Korean companies are, generally speaking, more rigidly hierarchical than their Western counterparts, with great emphasis placed on seniority. In private and public, Koreans are very deferential to elders, and society is very status-conscious. Though they were once regarded as impediments to Korean development, scholars now praise the Confucian work ethic and educational spirit as the keys to the nation's phenomenal economic growth over the last century.

Basic Beliefs

Like Buddhism, Confucianism is agnostic on the question of God. Confucianism's focus is not on the next world, but on this one. At its core is the belief that people, through learning and effort, can become virtuous. It places great emphasis on altruism, etiquette, and interpersonal relationships.

Confucianism ethics is based on three primary virtues: *ren* (altruism), *yi* (righteousness), and *li* (etiquette). *Ren* posits that you should treat others humanely—that you should do unto others as you would like them to do unto you. *Yi*, meanwhile, is the duty to uphold justice and righteousness, while *li* refers to etiquette and rituals.

One of the core concepts of Confucianism are the so-called "Five Relationships": king and subject, father and son, husband and wife, elder brother and younger brother, and friend and friend. These relationships carry with them prescribed responsibilities, most notably the duty of the junior party to respect the elder party, and for the elder party to treat the junior party well. The most typical—and, indeed, the most important—manifestation of this is the concept of filial piety, which extends to both one's living parents and deceased ancestors. Reverence of one's parents—and of social elders in general—is one of the most striking aspects of Korean society today.

The male ideal is the Confucian gentleman, the embodiment of personal virtue, integrity, and learning. In the context of

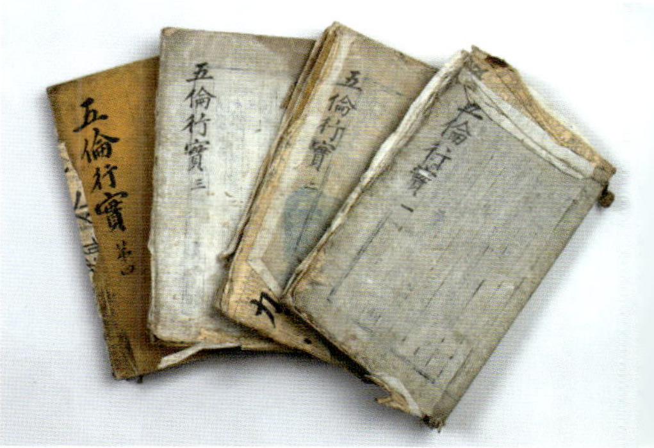

The *Oryunhaengsildo*, an illustrated book put together in 1797 to demonstrate examples of the so-called Five Relationships

Joseon Dynasty Korea, this was the *seonbi*, a scholar who had passed the civil service examination but shunned public office in favor of a life of study and personal cultivation.

Confucianism places great importance on learning—in Confucian society, you climbed the social ladder based on what you knew and how well you knew it. In China and Joseon Dynasty Korea, the most important manifestation of this was the Confucian civil service exam (*gwageo* in Korean), the passing of which opened the way to high office. A tiered system of Confucian schools opened throughout the country, aiming to instill Confucian values and prepare students for the exam. Modernizing reforms in the late 19th century did away with this system, but the culture of learning and test taking is still very much alive in Korea.

Confucian Practices

The most important Confucian tradition in contemporary Korea is the ancestral memorial rite, or *jesa*, a beautiful expression of filial piety for deceased ancestors. The most typical of these is the *gijesa*, which is held on the night before or the morning of the anniversary of an ancestor's death. Family members gather at the home of the eldest son. A shrine is created by placing the ancestor's memorial tablet on a low table. On the table are a variety of sacrificial foods. Male members of the family bow to the memorial tablet, after which the food is usually consumed by everyone who has gathered. Another memorial rite, the *charye*, is held on holidays such as Lunar New Year's Day and Chuseok, while another yet rite is held in autumn at the tombs of dead ancestors. During the Joseon Dynasty, these rites were performed for ancestors five generations back; nowadays, they are usually performed for just one or two generations. These Confucian rites are usually performed by

Various rites of the Jongmyo Daeje. The Jongmyo Daeje is a remembrance rite to the kings of the Joseon Dynasty held at Jongmyo Shrine, the kingdom's national shrine and now a UNESCO World Heritage Site.

Buddhists as well, but many Christians—Protestants in particular—abstain because of theological issues.

Another important rite is the Jongmyo Daeje, a royal memorial rite performed for deceased kings by the Joseon royal family at Jongmyo, a royal shrine in Seoul where the memorial tablets of the kings of Joseon are kept. It's a spectacular affair, accompanied by traditional court music and dance. During the Joseon Dynasty, it was performed five times a year, and it was considered vital to the peace and prosperity of the nation. Originally performed using music imported from China, the rite adopted in the 15th century Korean music written by King Sejong the Great. The dance features 84 female dancers in purple court attire.

Korea's monarchy has long since been abolished, but the Yi family—the royal clan of the Joseon Dynasty—still performs the rite on the first Sunday of May. The rite and its music have been designated Masterpieces of the Intangible Cultural Heritage of Humanity by UNESCO, and Jongmyo is listed as a UNESCO World Heritage Site.

THE SEOWON

One of the chief Confucian institutions of the Joseon Dynasty was the *seowon*. This institution served both as a Confucian shrine and a private academy for Confucian learning. It was usually established by a

A depiction of a typical class scene in a Joseon Dynasty *seowon* at the museum of Pilam Seowon

famed scholar, or the disciples or by family members of famed scholars, and accordingly it tended to serve as a base for a particular school of Confucian thought. The *seowon* sought to prepare students (almost always the sons of Korea's *yangban* class of scholar-aristocrats) for the *gwageo*, the Confucian civil service examination.

The most famous of these was Dosan Seowon in Andong, a grand complex on a wooded hillside in southeastern Korea. It was founded in 1575 by the disciples of famed Joseon scholar Yi Hwang, and for four centuries it did much to promote Yi's philosophy.

In 1871, the powerful prince regent of Joseon, Heungseon Daewongun, closed down most of Korea's *seowon* in a bid to strengthen royal control. Many have survived as shrines and museums, however, including Dosan Seowon, which until recently was prominently featured on the back of Korea's 1,000-won banknote.

Impact on Society

The impact Confucianism has had on Korean society cannot be overstated. Regardless of religious affiliation, almost all Koreans are influenced by the philosophy in one way or another. In short, Confucianism is hardwired into the culture.

The Confucian legacy can easily be seen in the enormous importance Koreans place on age, seniority, and status. This is visible in all areas of society, from the home to the office, and even on the subway. Koreans are especially respectful of the elderly, to their delight of older Western visitors to Korea. At the same time, many aspects of Korean society are very hierarchical. Korean corporate culture is especially so, with great importance attached to position and rank and the company president naturally sitting at the top.

The Confucian legacy is also reflected in Koreans' well-known love of education. Confucianism encouraged study, the pursuit of knowledge, and self-cultivation. Books and writing brushes were among the most prized possessions of a Joseon Dynasty gentleman. Today, Korean parents will go to incredible lengths to see that their children receive the best education possible. Students, meanwhile, are expected to study—the diligence of the Korean student is a subject of global admiration. Koreans also show tremendous respect for teachers and professors.

Many scholars also point to Confucianism as a factor in Korea's astounding economic growth in the last half of the 20th century, noting the philosophy's promotion of hard work, education, and social stability and organization.

Elementary school students learn Korean traditional culture and etiquette at a *seowon* during their summer vacation.

Jongga Ancestral Rituals and Food Culture

If Jongmyo is revered as the site of royal ancestral rites for the Joseon Dynasty, then the *jongga,* the shrines of individual clans which can be found scattered throughout Korea, might be even more meaningful in that they are attached to the homes where clan descendants continue to live till this day. Today's *jongga* are located in single-clan villages founded by distant ancestors from some 400 or 500 years ago. Ancient traditions remain alive, as evidenced by the number of traditional-style houses. For the memorial rites of the ancestors whose mortuary tablets are housed in the family shrine, protocol calls for the preparation of a variety of food items and the wearing of ritual attire. After the ancestral rites, the ritual foods are shared with neighbors, a community-minded gesture of the *jongga*. In the past, when ordinary Koreans struggled to eke out a livelihood, ritual food was a much-needed source of nutrition as well as a means of developing Korea's food culture.

Throughout the year, the *jongga* will perform a number of rituals, each with its own name. The basic rituals include an annual ritual on the eve of the anniversary of an ancestor's passing, a memorial ritual performed on the morning of the Lunar New Year and Chuseok holidays, and a tomb ritual held at the ancestor's tomb site. In addition, there is also an "immovable ancestral tablet" ritual, which is held to commemorate a distant ancestor who was commended for his extraordinary contributions to the welfare of the nation or his clan. In this case, an exception is made to the practice of housing the ancestral tablets of only the previous four generations: the mortuary tablet of this illustrious figure is permanently enshrined.

A Tour of Korea's Jongga Museums

Jongga literally means "head family or household," but this does not really help us understand the concept. It would be more accurate to say that *jongga* are households descended from a renowned ancestor through the eldest sons of the family. This could be the founder of a clan, but in most cases it is another ancestor who was honored in his time for some great deed or service, and who was granted what is known as an "immovable ancestral tablet" upon his death.

In addition to performing ancestral rituals, these *jongga* families also act as guardians of precious documents and artifacts handed down from one generation to the next. A few *jongga* families have taken this one step further and opened small museums or exhibition halls to display these treasures.

These small museums and their collections of artifacts and documents are precious treasure troves of Korean culture and history. Many of the artifacts, such as the oldest pair of eyeglasses in Korea, are the type of thing we have come to expect from museums. But the vast number of books, letters, royal edicts, and other documents preserved by these *jongga* came as a surprise. Nowhere else in the world will you find such large private collections of historical records. Some, of course, were vital in proving the pedigree of the *jongga*, but many are not. These collections can only be explained by the love these people held for the wisdom of their ancestors.

Herein lies the true value and importance of *jongga* museums: history here is not some abstract concept, but rather a living, breathing part of the family. And yet the number of *jongga* museums is very small compared to the number of *jongga* remaining in Korea. Even those who do stay in their ancestral homes often find it difficult to manage the vast collections of artifacts and documents, and so these treasures are often donated to other, larger museums. While it is fortunate that these treasures are being preserved, in a larger museum they are simply relics like any other, devoid of context.

Chunghyeon Museum, at the Jongga of Yi Won-ik

Chunghyeon Museum is very close to Seoul. There are very few *jongga* museums that remain intact in the capital region, and for good reason: unlike areas such as Andong, Seoul was hotly contested during the Korean War and many of the historical buildings in the area were destroyed. Fortunately, the *jongga* museum of Yi Won-ik (1547–1634) survived the war unscathed. Yi was a mid-Joseon Dynasty poet and high official. He served the government with distinction during the Imjin War of 1592–1598, and after the war, he was even appointed prime minister by King Gwanghaegun. His objections to the king's behavior earned him exile to the countryside, but when Gwanghaegun was deposed in a coup, Yi was brought back as prime minister by King Injo.

Unjanggak, at the Jongga of Kim Seong-il

Northwest of the city of Andong, on the road to Bongjeongsa Temple, is the *jongga* of Kim Seong-il. Kim Seong-il (1538–1593) was a well-known student of the famous Confucian scholar Toegye. He entered government service at the age of 30 and, in addition to holding various posts, traveled to China and Japan as a member of diplomatic missions.

A small museum called Unjanggak sits next to the house and contains some 20,000 artifacts and documents. It was originally built as a repository for the many relics and artifacts that have been handed down from generation to generation.

Sungwongak, at the Jongga of Kim Hyo-ro

Also in Andong, toward the Confucian academy of Dosan Seowon, a narrow road winds up and through a pine-covered hill, and suddenly the forest clears and a small traditional village appears. This is the Ocheon Historic Site, more commonly known as Gunja Village. It is also home to Sungwongak, the *jongga* museum of Kim Hyo-ro (1454–1534). Unlike many of the other *jongga* ancestors in the region, he shunned a life of government service and instead chose the quiet, untainted life of a scholar. The museum is built in a traditional style like the rest of the village, but is distinct in that it is a modern building made of cement. When the village was moved here in 1974, some 1,200 books and other documents were discovered in a small attic space above the rafters of Hujodang, a wooden structure that is 450 years old.

Mochunggwan, at the Jongga of General Nam I-heung

In the west coast town of Dangjin is Mochunggwan, the *jongga* museum of General Nam I-heung (1576–1627). General Nam lived in perilous times. When the Jurchen invaded Joseon, General Nam was charged with defending the Korean fortress town of Anju against an overwhelming force that outnumbered them by a factor of ten. Although he managed to hold off the invaders for some time, reinforcements sent to aid him turned around before reaching Anju the situation had been deemed hopeless. So General Nam opened up the gates of the fortress and let the enemy in—but his intention was not to surrender. Instead, he led the

Yeongmogak, at the Jongga of Ryu Seong-ryong

Andong's famous Hahoe Village is home to Yeongmogak, the small museum that houses the relics and artifacts from the *jongga* of Ryu Seong-ryong (1542–1607), who served as prime minister under King Seonjo (1567–1608) and was appointed supreme commander of the military forces when the Japanese invaded Korea in the 1590s. It is open to the public all year round. Exhibits include the *Record of Reprimand*, his most famous treatise, as well as other documents that have been preserved by the family from generation to generation. Many are records of events or other documents related to the Japanese invasions.

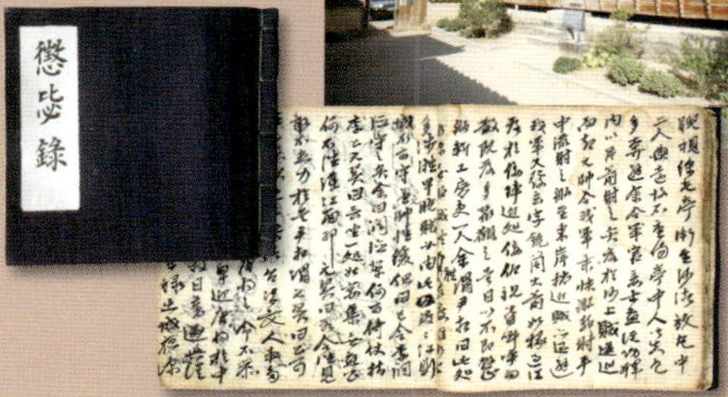

enemy troops to the magazine, where he ignited the gunpowder, killing both himself and many foes in a terrific explosion. When King Injo heard of his death, he grieved deeply and ordered that General Nam be given a state funeral.

4

Chapter Four

CHRISTIANITY

Spend any amount of time in Korea, and you'll soon discover the country's vibrant Christian community. The Seoul skyline is dotted by neon crosses fixed atop the city's countless churches. Several of the world's largest churches, including the 830,000-strong Yoido Full Gospel Church, are located here. It's estimated that about 28% of Korea's population is Christian (18% Protestant, 10% Catholic)—the second highest percentage in Asia after the Philippines. In terms of enthusiasm, however, Korean Christians are second to none. In fact, according to recent news reports, Korean churches dispatch the second largest number of Christian missionaries abroad (behind only the United States), a stunning accomplishment given Korea's small population.

Christianity has played an important role in Korea's contemporary history, particularly during the colonial period, when Christians were prominent in the nationalist movement, and in the post-

Liberation era, when Christians contributed greatly to the Korean democratization movement. Six of Korea's ten presidents have been Protestant or Catholic Christians, including the last four.

History

Korean Christianity might have a vibrant present, but it wasn't always that way. In the late 17th century, works by the Italian Jesuit missionary Matteo Ricci were first brought to Korea through royal tribute missions. By the latter half of the next century, reformist scholars had established a church led by a system of lay clergy. It was an almost unparalleled experience in the history of Catholicism —a church establishing itself without the help of foreign missionaries.

Nicolas Cheong Jin-suk and the priests of the Seoul Archdiocese

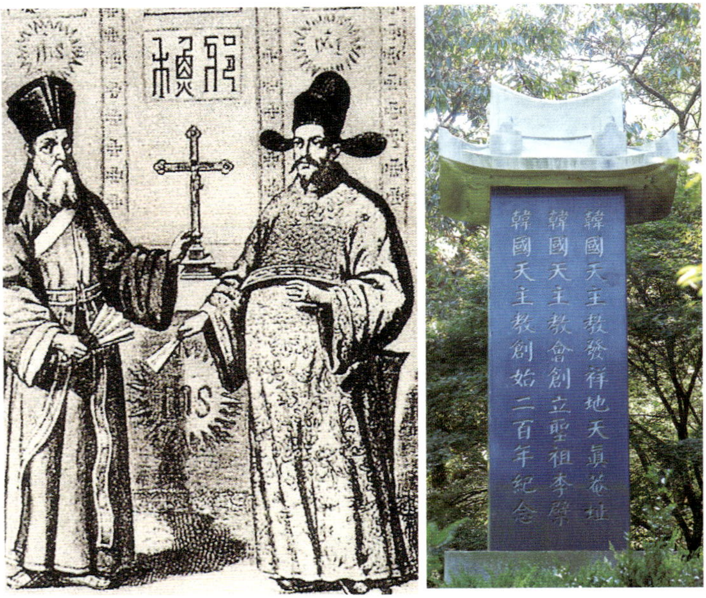

(Left) Italian Jesuit missionary and scholar Matteo Ricci, who had a profound influence on the founding of Korean Catholicism
(Right) Memorial for the founding of Korean Catholicism. Located in Gwangju, this spot represents the indigenous emergence of Catholicism after scholars of the Namin faction began studying Catholic texts in the 18th century.

The new faith was viewed with abject horror by Korea's Confucian establishment, however, and Catholicism underwent several bloody persecutions throughout the 19th century. Many Catholics were killed, and those who survived often fled to remote mountain villages, where they established small communities of believers far from the persecution in the cities. Not even Western missionaries were immune—in the great persecution of 1866, for example, nine French priests were executed, sparking an armed conflict with France.

By comparison, Protestantism came later, and consequently had a much easier time of things. Catholics were forced for over a century to pray and proselytize illegally, often at great risk to life and limb, but Protestant missionaries from the United States, Canada, Great Britain, and Australia entered Korea in the late 19th century as diplomats, doctors, and educators, often with the support of the royal authorities, who viewed them as agents of modernization. Indeed, Protestant missionaries played an important role in Korea's modernization, setting up many of the country's first modern hospitals, schools, and universities (and, of course, churches).

Korean Christianity went through a rough patch under Japanese imperial rule. The Japanese distrusted the Western missionaries (most of whom were expelled at the start of the Pacific War) and viewed the churches—many of which had become centers of anti-Japanese nationalist activities—with suspicion. Still, at least until the 1930s, the religion continued to flourish. Christian activity in northern Korea was so vibrant, in fact, that the city of Pyongyang (ironically enough, now the capital of atheist North Korea) was called the "Jerusalem of the East."

(Left) Missionaries, nurses and trainee nurses pose for a photograph in front of Korea's first nursing school in 1908.
(Right) The Gwanghyewon, or "Widespread Relief House." This was Korea's first modern hospital, established in Seoul's Jae-dong district in 1885.

(Above) President Kim Young-sam, a Protestant Christian, at service (Below) President Kim Dae-jung, a Catholic, at mass

Liberation from colonial rule, post-war economic development, and Korea's close relationship with the United States provided the environment for a second boom in Korean Christianity. The number of Protestants jumped from just over 623,000 in 1960 to over 8 million in 2005. Their influence on society grew, too—of Korea's post-Liberation presidents, three (Syngman Rhee, Kim Young-sam, and Lee Myung-bak) have been Protestants and two (Kim Dae-jung and Roh Moo-hyun) have been Catholic. In particular, Christians played a major role in Korea's democratization movement of the 1970s and 1980s.

The Great Persecutions

When Catholicism first entered Korea in the 18th century, it was met with a good deal of hostility from Korea's ruling Neo-Confucian elite, who viewed the foreign faith as dangerous heresy. King Yeongjo officially declared the faith illegal in 1758, and the first persecution of Catholics began in 1785. At first, the persecutions were quite mild—usually, only the owner of a particular meeting house would be punished with exile, while believers of noble birth were simply pressured to renounce their faiths.

In 1791, several Catholic noblemen directly challenged the

Haemi Martyrdom Holy Ground, Seosan. This site marks the spot where countless Catholics from the Korean interior were martyred during the four great persecutions of the 19th century.

government by not only refusing to renounce their faith, but also refusing to perform the crucially important Neo-Confucian ancestral rites and burning their ancestral memorial tablets. To the Confucianist, such a violation of filial piety was an unforgivable outrage. The nobles were immediately executed, sending a chilling message to the Church. In terms of scale, the incident was relatively minor, but it served as a taste of things to come.

The 19th century witnessed no fewer than four persecutions of Catholics in Korea. When King Jeongjo, who had been relatively lenient with the Catholics, died in 1800, he was succeeded by his young son King Sunjo. His grandmother, Queen Jeongsun, ruled as dowager. In 1801, the dowager launched a persecution of Catholics as part of a larger war against her factional enemies. Some 400 Catholics were executed, and another 400 exiled. During the

1

2

1. Jindumbeong at Haemi Martyrdom Holy Ground. During the persecutions, Catholics had their arms tied and were thrown head-first into the pond to drown.
2. Kim Dae-geon (1822–1846), Korea's first Catholic priest. He was canonized by Pope John Paul II in 1984.
3. Catholic Holy Site at Ganghwado's Gapgotjin, where Cahtolics were executed during the great persecution of 1866
4. Relics from Catholic martyrs kept at the memorial hall of Jeoldusan Martyrs Grounds

3

4
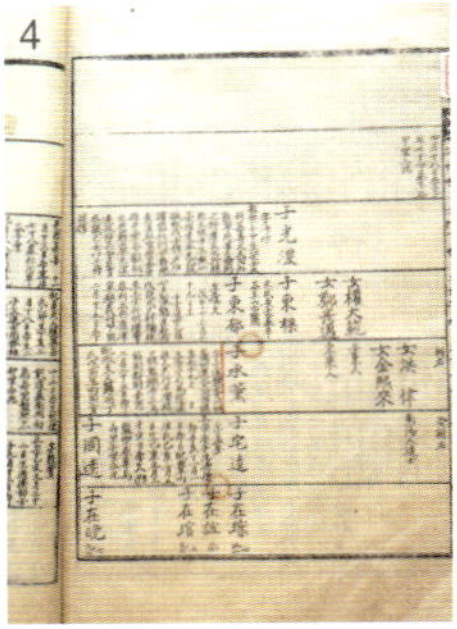

persecution, one Catholic noble attempted to send a silk letter to the French bishop in Beijing, describing the persecution and begging for Western warships to be sent to Korea. The letter was intercepted, however, and Catholics—who now appeared to be traitors, too—were subjected to further persecution.

The next persecution came in 1839. This, too, began as a factional struggle between two powerful families, the Andong Kim clan and the Pungyang Jo clan. In 1834, the Jo clan seized control over the royal court from the Kim clan. Anti-Catholic in nature, the Jo-dominated court of Kim Heonjeong blamed the Kim clan for being soft on Catholics and launched a persecution, killing hundreds of Catholics, including three French missionary priests. Meanwhile, another persecution in 1846 claimed the life of St. Andrew Kim Taegon, the first Korean-born Catholic priest.

The last of the persecutions—and by far the bloodiest—came in 1866. This persecution came against a backdrop of growing imperial aggression in East Asia. In 1860, British and French forces brought the Second Opium War to a close by routing the Chinese and sacking the Summer Palace in Beijing. China was forced to sign a series of humiliating "unequal treaties" with the Western powers. Japan, too, had been forcefully opened up to Western trade, and Southeast Asia was coming under Western imperial control. In Korea, the Russians were encroaching from the north, and French missionary priests were illegally smuggling themselves into the country.

Korea's conservative prince regent, Heungseon Daewongun, ultimately decided the best way to defend Korea was to keep the country hermetically closed. In 1866, he launched a vicious persecution of Korea's growing Catholic community. Nine French priests were arrested and executed, along with 40 Korean converts. When word of this got back to the French, they responded with a naval expedition against the strategic island of Ganghwado. Not long after, a Western adventurer attempted to raid the tomb of Heungseon Daewongun's ancestor, and the US Navy launched a raid of its own on Ganghwado after an American trade ship was burned and its crew killed after it had illegally sailed up the Daedonggang River to Pyongyang. The Western attacks led Heungseon Daewongun to intensify his persecution of Catholics. The persecution ended when the regent turned over power to his son, King Gojong, in 1873. By that time, about 8,000 Korean Catholics—half the country's Catholic believers—were dead. It wouldn't be until Korea and France signed a diplomatic relations accord in 1886 that Catholics gained the freedom to practice their faith openly.

In May 1984, Pope John Paul II canonized 103 martyrs of the Korean persecutions in a ceremony in Seoul. Among those canonized were St. Andrew Kim Taegon and the French priests martyred in the persecutions.

Missionaries

At the end of the 19th century, Protestant missionaries from the United States, Great Britain, Canada, and Australia began missions in Korea following its opening to the West. In addition to their religion, these missionaries also brought social and political change —Christians were at the forefront of improving the position of women in Korean society, for instance, and many Christians were active in the independence struggle against the Japanese.

One of the most enduring contributions of Western missionaries was the creation of modern schools and universities. Many of the first missionaries were educators in addition to preachers, setting up many of Korea's first high schools and universities. Yonsei University and Ewha Womans University, both elite higher education institutions today, are just two examples.

East Hall of Pai Chai Hakdang, Korea's first modern intermediate school

The missionaries passed on not only their faith to the Koreans, but their missionary zeal as well. Korea now dispatches the second largest number of Christian missionaries overseas, after the United States. In 2004, there were 12,000 Korean missionaries working in 160 nations; by 2009, that number was up to 20,000. Korean missionaries are especially active in countries and regions—such as the Middle East—that have been traditionally hostile to Western missionary work. In this, Korean missionaries have a distinct advantage—unlike their Western counterparts, they come from a nation with no imperial baggage, and their non-Western backgrounds help them better engage with non-Western audiences, particularly those in Asia.

Christianity and the Nationalist and Democracy Movements

Korean independence activists Seo Jae-pil and Ahn Chang-ho, who were both Protestants. They served together in the Independence Club, and published Korea's first privately owned newspaper.

Unlike in other formerly colonized nations where Christianity was usually affiliated with the colonial regime, Christianity in Korea came to be strongly associated with the Korean independence movement against Japanese colonial rule. One indication of this is that 16 of the 33 nationalist representatives who issued the Korean Declaration of Independence of 1919, kicked off the milestone March 1 Independence Movement, were Christian.

The fact that Korea was colonized not by a Christian Western power but by the non-Christian Japanese is at least partly responsible for the religion's fortunate associations. Indeed, Japanese colonial policy itself forced Christians into a leadership role in the resistance. For example, the colonial authorities in the 1920's attempted to force Koreans to pray at Shinto shrines, prompting outrage and protests from angered Christians.

Just as importantly, Christianity in Korea had become closely associated with more modern and progressive social, cultural, and political ideas, including democracy and self-determination. Korean Christians kept up the fight against Japanese attempts to assimilate Korea culturally, most importantly by keeping the language alive. Korean churches were active promoters of Korean language education and Korea's unique Hangeul writing system: the Bible and other religious works were almost always translated or written in Korean.

Korea's political activism did not end with the nation's liberation

A candlelight vigil after a special mass
for the labor rights of Korea in 1995

from colonial rule in 1945. Korean Christians would again take the lead in efforts to bring democracy to the country in the decades following the Korean War. In this struggle, the role of the Catholic Church—which had remained relatively passive compared to its Protestant cousins during the colonial period—was especially important. Under the leadership of Cardinal Stephen Kim Sou-hwan, the Korean Catholic Church took an active interest in democratization and labor rights. In 1974, the Catholic Priests

Korean Megachurches: Yoido Full Gospel Church

As of 2007, five of the world's ten biggest megachurches were in Korea. And of these, none is as mega-big as Seoul's Yoido Full Gospel Church. Founded by Pastor David Yonggi Cho and his future mother-in-law in 1958, the church is now the world's largest, with a congregation of nearly one million. Not bad for a church that began with a congregation of just six under a used U.S. Marine Corps tent. Its main assembly hall in Seoul's Yeouido district (the so-called "Korean Manhattan") can hold up to 12,000, which is not nearly enough come Sunday. The Economist described the church thusly:

> *Each of the seven Sunday services at Yoido is a logistical challenge: apart from the 12,000 people in the main sanctuary, another 20,000 follow the service on television in overflow chapels scattered around neighbouring buildings. Some 38,000 children go to Sunday school during the day. As one service begins and the next ends, around 60,000 comers and goers are ushered by white-jacketed traffic directors. If you want to attend one of the two services starring the church's founder, David Cho, you need to be an hour early or you won't get in.*
>
> *Not that you will lack entertainment whilst you wait. The massed choir*

Association for Justice was formed after the arrest of Bishop Daniel Tji Hak-soon, bishop of Wonju, for pro-democracy activities. Seoul's Myeong-dong Cathedral, the mother church of Korean Catholicism, became a haven for political dissidents; even today, it is considered a holy ground of Korean democracy.

Korean churches, both Protestant and Catholic, remain active in Korea's social, economic and political issues, including the environment, workers' rights, and North Korean human rights.

(one of 12) is already belting out hymns, backed by a large orchestra (one of three). The audience sings along, with huge television screens supplying the words, karaoke style. Pictures of the service are beamed to hundreds of satellite churches around the world and to Prayer Mountain, a gruelling religious camp close to the border with the North. Translation is offered in English, Japanese, Chinese, Spanish, French, Indonesian, Malay and Arabic.

Experts point to several reasons for the success of megachurches in Korea. One is Koreans' well-known communitarianism. Culturally, Koreans like to do things in groups, and this applies to going to church, too. Megachurches have also successfully used "cells"—often led by women—to virally market church membership.

Korean megachurches are typically led by charismatic preachers. In this, they differ little from megachurches in the United States and elsewhere. That such churches have succeeded so well in Korea, however, points to a unique feature of the Korean religious landscape. Prior to the introduction of Christianity, Confucianism, and Buddhism, Korea was a shamanist nation (see Chapter 2), a cultural legacy that created fertile ground for charismatic preachers.

Anglicanism in Korea

Anglicanism came to Korea in 1890, when British naval chaplain Charles John Corfe established a church in what is now Incheon. The church is still standing, a handsome stone chapel not far from Incheon's Jayu Park. Anglican missionaries were especially active in the Gyeonggi-do area and some parts of the Chungcheong-do region, where they established not only churches but modern schools and hospitals, too. One of Korea's first Western hospitals, in fact, was established in Incheon in 1891 by Eli Barr Landis, a young American Anglican missionary doctor who came to Korea with Bishop Corfe. As of 2001, the church had 63,973 believers.

Anglicanism displayed a remarkable ability to "indigenize" upon its arrival on Korean shores. Several of Korea's oldest Anglican churches are *hanok* churches, built in Korean traditional fashion. There is no better example of this than the beautiful Ganghwa Anglican Church. Also known as Saints Peter and Paul Anglican Church, Ganghwa Anglican Church first opened in 1893. The current church was consecrated by Bishop Corfe in 1900. King Gojong lent the missionaries a palace woodcutter who had participated in the 1867 reconstruction of Gyeongbokgung Palace. The result was a splendid church marrying royal palace style with Buddhist and Western

Rectory, Ganghwa Anglican Church

Seoul Anglican Cathedral

architectural elements. The layout of the church ground, with its gates and bell pavilion, is quite similar to that of a Korean Buddhist temple. The colorful paint, roof spines, and gargoyles recall Korean official buildings such as one might see at one of Seoul's royal palaces. The interior, meanwhile, is a *hanok* interpretation of the Western basilica.

The gem of Korean Anglicanism, however, is Seoul Anglican Cathedral, widely regarded as one of Seoul's most stunning pieces of architecture. Consecrated in 1926, it's a Romanesque cathedral with elements of Korean traditional architecture, best illustrated by the windows and roof. Despite its very exotic features, it still harmonizes with nearby Deoksugung Palace, owing to the care that went into its design. Only 50% complete when it was consecrated, the cathedral stood in truncated form for about 70 years. In 1993, however, a British tourist visiting the cathedral noted that he'd seen Dixon's original plans at the library at which he worked. Dixon's plans thus rediscovered, work was undertaken to complete the cathedral as originally intended. The expansion, which gave the church its current Latin Cross shape, was completed in 1996.

5

Chapter Five

OTHER RELIGIONS

In addition to shamanism, Buddhism, Confucianism, and Christianity, the Korean religious landscape is also home to a number of smaller faiths. This includes both indigenous ones like Cheondogyo and Won Buddhism, as well as overseas faiths like Islam. Their presence is further evidence of Korea's rich and tolerant religious tapestry.

CHEONDOGYO

Cheondogyo, or "Religion of the Heavenly Way," is probably Korea's largest and best-known indigenous faith. A product of the Donghak movement of the late 19th century, the religion was based on Confucianism, but incorporated elements of other Korean faiths as well, including Taoism, Buddhism, and even Christianity.

Although a relatively minor faith today, with its faithful

numbering less than 1% of the population, it had a more prominent presence in the early part of the 20th century. The religion produced many leaders of the Korean independence movement, for which reason the faith is closely associated with Korean nationalism. In the 1920s, it had as many as three million adherents, but the number is now believed to be a mere 100,000.

History

The late 19th century was a dramatic—and traumatic—time in Korean history. The Western imperialists had humiliated neighboring China, and their missionaries were threatening the old ways. In Japan, Western warships had opened the country to foreign trade, prompting a wholesale social and political revolution. Korea, too, was coming under imperial pressure from Western

Cheondogyo Seminary

(Left) Choe Je-u, the founder Donghak Movement
(Right) Choe Si-hyeong, the second leader of the Donghak Movement

powers, China and, increasingly, Japan. Internally, Korean society was torn asunder by factional disputes within the ruling Neo-Confucian elite, and the foreign faith of Catholicism continued to gain adherents despite several official persecutions. All the while, the Korean peasantry suffered under exploitation and corruption.

This was in such a context that a young Confucian scholar by the name of Choe Je-u founded the Donghak ("Eastern Learning") movement in the 1860s. Donghak was a comprehensive approach to Korea's traditional philosophical and spiritual heritage, based largely on Confucianism but incorporating elements of Buddhism and other religions, too. Its primary goal was to create a new, more just world. To make it easy for the peasantry to understand, Choe set his teachings to music.

Donghak was bitterly opposed to government corruption and the growing foreign influence in Korea. The government saw Choe as a threat and a heretic; he was arrested in 1863 and executed the following year. His successor Choe Si-hyeong, however, kept his teachings alive. He worked to systematize the faith, which was gaining popularity amongst Korea's hard-pressed peasants despite official persecution. In 1894, followers launched the Donghak Peasant

Revolt, two full-scale peasant uprisings that were put down amid much bloodshed by an alliance of loyalist forces and Japanese troops. After several years on the run, Choe was captured and executed for his role in the uprising, but not before naming as his successor Son Byeong-hui, who had served as a commander during the revolt.

In the spirit of the times, Son went to work trying to modernize Donghak. But as Korea was too dangerous an environment for a

A painting of the Donghak Peasant Revolt, a peasant uprising led by the Donghak Movement, which criticized the Joseon Dynasty's feudal society as oppressive and irrational.

man with his record, he went into exile in Japan, where he associated with other reformist-minded Korean exiles and witnessed post-Meiji modernization in action. From there, he launched a reform movement to modernize Donghak, even going so far as to change the faith's name to Cheondogyo. Reformists cut their hair

The painting of the reading of the Korean Declaration of Independence, displayed at Cheonan Independence Hall. Proclaimed on March 1, 1919, the document was signed by 33 independence activists, 15 of whom were members of Cheondogyo.

and took to wearing simpler, more modern garb.

In 1905, he returned to Korea, where he continued to work on modernizing his faith and Korean society at large. This work became even more important after Japan's annexation of Korea in 1910: in his view, Korean society needed to strengthen itself in order for the nation to recover its independence. Cheondogyo's nationwide organization, along with associated businesses like printing, also allowed it to promote nationalism and independence ideals under the nose of the Japanese. Futhermore, Son formed alliances with other religious groups, most notably Christians and Buddhists, to promote his modernist and nationalist agenda.

Cheondogyo's big moment came on March 1, 1919. On that day, thirty-three nationalist representatives gathered in a restaurant in Seoul's Insa-dong neighborhood to read the Korean Declaration of Independence. Of these representatives, fifteen were Cheondogyo adherents, and copies of the declaration had even been printed up by a Cheondogyo printing company. The reading of the Korean Declation of Independence sparked the March 1 Independence Movement, one of the landmark events of Korean contemporary history.

Basic Beliefs

Like Confucianism, Cheondogyo is primarily concerned with this world, not the next. It seeks to create an earthly paradise by achieving peace and virtue and reforming obsolete practices. Its primary belief is that "Man and God are one." According to Cheondogyo, there is a God, who is venerated as Hanullim, or "Master Heaven," but this God is more an embodiment of justice and virtue than an actual deity. Also like Confucianism, Cheondogyo places much emphasis on personal cultivation.

Cheondogyo Central Temple & Bonghwaggak Monastery

An Insa-dong landmark, the Cheondogyo Central Temple is one of Korea's most beautiful pieces of contemporary architecture. Conceived by Cheondogyo leader and independence activist Son Byeong-hui, who was one of the leaders of the March 1 Independence Movement, construction of the hall began in 1918 and was completed in 1921. The grand structure was designed by Japanese colonial architect Nakamura Yoshihei, but given the building's distinctive Vienna Secession style, it is likely that Anton Feller, an Austrian architect in Nakamura's employ, had a hand in the design. Built as a deliberate challenge to Myeong-dong Cathedral, the temple was one of Seoul's three largest buildings at the time of its construction. Its beautiful Art

(Left) The Bonghwanggak, the institution produced Cheondogyo leaders who led the independence movement under Japanese colonial rule (Right) Cheondogyo Central Temple

Nouveau interior, decorated with symbols of Korean nationalism, is made all the more amazing by the lack of pillars to hold up the massive roof—a revolutionary design in Korea at that time.

The temple's construction was financed with donations from believers. Most of the donations, however, went into funding the March 1 Independence Movement.

Another Cheondogyo holy site is Bonghwaggak Monastery, on the lower slopes of Bukhansan National Park northwest of Seoul. The Korean-style house was built in 1911 at Son's direction to serve as a place for training leaders.

Won Buddhism

Won Buddhism, or "Round Buddhism," is an indigenous form of reformed Buddhism that developed in Korea in the 20th century. It seeks to bring traditional Buddhism into the modern period by making its teachings and practices relevant to contemporary life. Its goal is to build a single world community and realize the oneness of life based on the Buddhist world view of interdependence and interconnectedness.

Park Chung-bin, the founder of Won Buddhism

Won Buddhism was founded by Park Chung-bin (better known by his Buddhist name of Sotaesan), who attained enlightenment at the age of 26 in 1916. Upon attaining enlightenment, he declared, "All things are of a single body and nature; all dharmas are of a single root source. In this regard, the Way (Tao) that is free from arising nor ceasing and the principle of the retribution and response of cause and

Female clergy of Cheondogyo in meditation

effect, being mutually grounded on each other, have formed a clear and rounded framework."

Won Buddhism shares with traditional Buddhism many basic principles and practices, including the use of Seon (Zen) meditation. Where Won Buddhism parts ways with mainstream Buddhism is in its concern with the secular world. Won Buddhism accepts material society as a given, but seeks to develop man's spirituality in accordance with the development of a materialistic, technologically advanced, and globalized civilization. Won Buddhism also stresses female participation, including within the religion's leadership, and embraces inter-faith dialogue.

Il Won Sang

The Il Won Sang is the circular symbol of the Dharmakaya Buddha and the Buddha Nature of all beings, and is the chief icon of Won Buddhism. In the faith, the Buddha's image is replaced by this symbol, which represents the mind image of the Buddha rather than his physical form. Unlike the physical form, the circle represents the Buddha's infinite mind-essence, combining both being and nonbeing and sustaining itself through past, present, and future. This makes it the original source of all things.

Won Buddhism's prayer for peace

Fourfold Grace

In Won Buddhism, grace is an expression of interdependency and interconnectedness—nothing in the universe can exist in and by itself, and each being in the universe is related to and indebted to other beings for its existence. The Fourfold Grace refers to the Grace of Heaven and Earth, the Grace of Parents, the Grace of Fellow Beings, and the Grace of Laws. In the words of Sotaesan himself:

> *The way is to believe in the Truth of Il Won Sang as our object of faith and pray for all blessings and happiness from the Truth. Il Won Sang is composed of the Fourfold Grace, which is comprised of all things in the universe. All things that we see in the universe are nothing but buddhas. Therefore, at all times and in all places we must be very respectful and cautious toward all things, keeping a pure and a pious manner as if we were before the real Buddha. We should also make buddha offerings directly to all things in which we are involved, thereby creating blessings and happiness in your everyday life. In a word, this is the way to turn a partial faith into a well-rounded and complete faith, and a superstitious faith into a realistic faith.*

(Source: Official Site of Won Buddhism)

Holy Site: Won Buddhism Headquarters

Won Buddhism's headquarters is located in the small town of Iksan in southwest Korea. The headquarters was founded in 1924 and represents a treasure trove of period architecture from the 1920s, 1930s and 1940s. It's also home to a pagoda holding relics of Won Buddhism's founder, Sotaesan.

DAEJONGGYO

Daejonggyo, or "Religion of the Great Ancestor," was founded in 1909 by Na Cheol, a teacher and Korean independence activist. It worships as a god Dangun, the legendary founder of the Korean people. As one might expect, the religion is closely associated with the Korean independence movement. It isn't a widely practiced faith—there were, just 10,000 Koreans adherents in 1995—but it is nonetheless the largest of the "Dangun" religions, of which there are several.

According to Na, Daejonggyo was a revival of a Goguryeo (37 BC—AD 668) faith that posited its own holy trinity: Hwanin the creator, Hwanung the teacher, and Dangun the teacher. The basic tenet of the faith is to worship God, respect one's ancestors, and love one's fellow man. The religion claims to be 4,000 years old.

During the colonial period, the faith's adherents were persecuted, and many fled to

Dangun: The Founder of Daejonggyo

Since time immemorial, the Korean people have taken Dangun to be the king of the "God-Human Being." His divinity is said to connote a trinity—the God-Father, the God-Teacher, and the God-King of the universe—and thus a unitarian God, while his humanity is seen as suggesting the trinity of the threefold essence in human relations (father, teacher, and king), and thus the supreme man. For this reason, he is called by the name of Hanbae-Geum, or the "God-Human Being-King." "Haneol," the divinity of Dangun, means the trinity of three gods, while "Hanbae-Geom," the humanity of Dangun, means the trinity of the threefold essence in human relations. Another of the Daejonggyo ideals is to have every person learn and follow the teachings of Dangun in order to finally become a god-man like Dangun, who is viewed, in a sense, an immortal wizard.

Ancient Korean texts hold that Dangun was born on the third day of the tenth month in the year 2457 B.C., and that from that day forward he traveled the country teaching the people of god, the way, and the principles of human relations until the same day of the same month in the year 2333 B.C., 125 years after his birth, when he first founded the country. The ancestors of modern-day Koreans regarded the tenth lunar month as first among all months and designated its third day to be "World-Opening Day." The ritual of worshiping heaven and ancestors by preparing various offerings was performed in that month for thousands of years in Korea.

Manchuria. In 1916, Na—frustrated with the situation—martyred himself by committing suicide at a shrine on Mt. Guwolsan in northern Korea. After his death, leadership passed on to a number of other teachers.

Photo taken after the Battle of Cheongsan-ri, in which Korean independence forces defeated a Japanese force. The Koreans were led by Gen. Kim Jwa-jin, a leader of the Daejonggyo faith.

Indeed, the practice is still observed in rural areas of Korea to this day, and the Republic of Korea, ever adopted the calendar of the Dangi period, which starts from the national founding year in 2333 B.C., after its liberlation in 1945. Its use continued until the adoption of the Gregorian calendar. October 3 remains a national holiday.

After founding the country, Dangun Hanbae-geom is said to have ruled five tribes: the Hoang, Balg, Hyeon, Jegg, and Nam. He is described as a peaceful leader who instructed them in the "five teachings": the nature of the universe, the unitarian god (Haneol), the universe, the world, and truth. He also took responsibility for five types of human affairs: food, order, disease, punishment, and morality. On March 15, 2240 B.C., after 93 years of wise rule, he is said to have ascended to heaven from the top of Mt. Hanbalg (today's Mt. Baekdusan), bequeathing the throne to his first son Buru.

(Source: Official Site of Daejonggyo)

Islam in Korea

Seoul Central Masjid

Korea has a small but flourishing Muslim community. There are currently about 35,000 Muslims in Korea. Thirty thousand of which are Koreans. The remainder are foreigners largely from Muslim nations in the Middle East and South and Southeast Asia.

Islam was introduced (or reintroduced) to Korea during the Korean War, when Turkish troops sent to Korea to fight under the UN flag introduced their faith to the local population. Early converts established Korea's first mosque in 1955. The number of Muslims in Korea got an additional boost in the 1970s, when thousands of Koreans were sent to the Middle East to work on construction projects during the petrodollar boom. Some of these workers converted to Islam and brought their faith back with them when they returned to Korea. It was in 1976 that the most prominent symbol of Korean Islam—the landmark Seoul Central Mosque in the Itaewon neighborhood—was built.

Korea's history with Islam goes back much further, however. Korea's first contacts with the Muslim world took place during the Unified Silla period (668–935), when Arabs and Persian traders came to Korea. Following the establishment of the Goryeo Dynasty (918–1392), the Muslim presence in Korea would reach new heights. Arab traders flooding into the Goryeo, and in the late Goryeo period, when Korea was dominated by the Mongol Yuan Dynasty, Muslims came to Korea as soldiers and administrators, and the Muslim faith came putting down roots in the country.

These Muslims, especially the ones who settled in Korea, played a leading role in bridging the gap between Koreans and the Mongols. Muslims formed a community just outside the Goryeo capital of Gaegyeong, where they built a mosque for daily prayers. Under an imam, they also performed a group prayer ritual called the "Daejohoesongchuk" at the royal court under an imam, and they burned incense for the king in their shrines. Muslims were also entrusted with raising falcons, which were sent to the Yuan court as tribute. Central Asian tradesmen encouraged international trade, bring Goryeo closer to the world.

APPENDIX

OTHER INFORMATION

STATISTICS ON RELIGION BY POPULATION IN KOREA

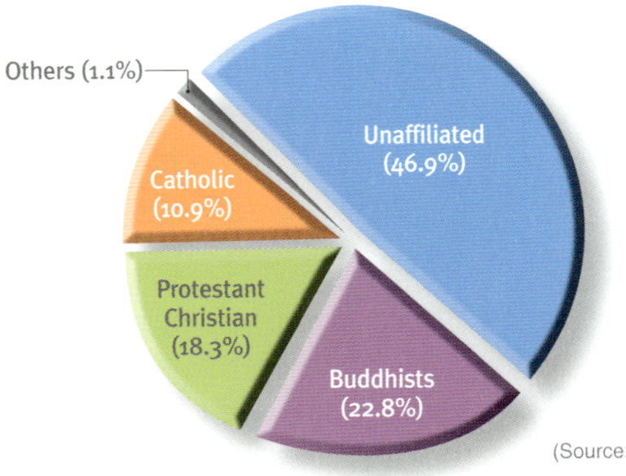

(Source: KOSIS Database)

In Korea's last household census in 2005, over half of Koreans reported some sort of religious affiliation, while 46.9% identified themselves as unaffiliated. Some 22.8% identified as Buddhists, 18.3% identified as Protestant Christian, and 10.9% identified as Catholic. One percent identified as "other," which includes a wide range of less common faiths, from indigenous religions like Cheondogyo and Won Buddhism to faiths from overseas like Islam and Baha'i.

More about Religion in Korea

ON RELIGION IN GENERAL:

James H. Grayson, *Korea - A Religious History*, London: Routledge, 2002

Don Baker, *Korean Spirituality*, Honolulu: University of Hawaii Press, 2008

ON SHAMANISM:

Richard W. I. Guisso, *Shamanism: The Spirit World of Korea*, Fremont: Jain Publishing Company, Inc., 1988

Kim Tae-gon, *Korean Shamanism*, Seoul: Royal Asiatic Society Korean Branch, 2008

ON BUDDHISM:

Lewis R. Lancaster & Chai-Shin Yu, *Introduction of Buddhism to Korea: New Cultural Patterns*, Fremont: Jain Publishing Company, Inc., 1989

Sung-woo Kim, *Buddhist Architecture of Korea*, Seoul: Hollym, 2007

ON CONFUCIANISM:

Kang Jae-eun, *The Land of Scholars: Two Thousands Years of Korean Confucianism*, Paramus: Homa & Sekey Books, 2005

Song Hye-jin, *Confucian Ritual Music of Korea*, Seoul: The Korea Foundation, 2008

ON CHRISTIANITY:

Chai-Shin Yu, *Korea and Christianity*, Fremont: Asian Humanities Press, 2004

Robert E., Jr. Buswell & Timothy S. Lee, *Christianity in Korea*, Honolulu: University of Hawaii Press, 2007

7 Buddhist Temples

1

2

1. Jogyesa

While not Korea's oldest or largest temple, this small monastery in the heart of Seoul is the head temple of the Jogye Order of Korean Buddhism, Korea's dominant Buddhist order.

2. Bulguksa

A UNESCO World Heritage Site along with nearby Seokguram Grotto, Bukguksa is considered the gem of Silla temple architecture. The pagodas in its main courtyard and stone steps are considered especially beautiful.

3. Buseoksa

Founded in 676 by the great Silla monk Uisang, Buseoksa occupies a dramatic location on the slopes of Mt. Sobaeksan. Its main hall, reached by a flight of 108 steps, dates back to 1376, making it one of the oldest wooden buildings in Korea.

4. Songgwangsa

This monastery in southwest Korea is considered one of the "Three Jewels" of Korean Buddhism, along with Tongdosa and Haeinsa (see below). Songgwangsa is known as one of Korea's foremost Zen training centers.

5. Tongdosa

Located in the mountains just north of Busan, Tongdosa is a sprawling temple with a very large and active community of monks. It is home to relics of the actual Buddha, making it a very special place indeed.

6. Haeinsa

A UNESCO World Heritage Site, Haeinsa is home to the *Tripitaka Koreana*, the most complete collection of woodblock prints of the Buddhist canon in Chinese characters.

7. Beopjusa

Hidden in the foothills of Mt. Songnisan in central Korea, this beautiful and grand monastery is blessed with some of Korea's finest works of religious architecture, including one of Korea's few remaining wooden pagoda-like structures.

7 Confucian Sites

1. Jongmyo Shrine

This UNESCO World Heritage Site in Seoul is where the memorial tablets of the kings of Joseon Dynasty are enshrined. It hosts the Jongmyo Jerye memorial rite every May.

2. Seonggyungwan Mumyo Shrine

One of Seoul's hidden gems, this Confucian shrine is located on the campus of Sungkyunkwan University.

3. Dosan Seowon

A spectacular and well-preserved Confucian academy, Dosan Seowon was founded in 1549 by students of renowned Confucian scholar Yi Hwang.

4. Sosu Seowon

The first seowon, or private Confucian academy, established in Korea, Sosu Seowon has a history that dates back to 1542.

5. Byeongsan Seowon

Not far from Andong's Hahoe Village, Byeongsan Seowon blends seamlessly with the surrounding mountains and rivers.

6. Huwon Garden

Widely praised as the most spectacular example of Korean gardening anywhere, the gardens of Changdeokgung Palace also reveal much about the worldview of Joseon Dynasty Korea.

7. Soswaewon Garden

Hidden in a bamboo grove in southwest Korea, this pleasure garden is a wonderful example of Confucian rustic beauty.

5

7

7 Christian Sites

1

3

1. Myeong-dong Cathedral

Completed in 1898, this beautiful Gothic cathedral in the heart of Seoul is not only the heart of Korean Catholicism, but also a symbol of Korea's democracy movement of the 1980s.

2. Jeoldusan Martyrs Grounds

This memorial site on a hill overlooking the Hangang River marks where countless Korean Catholics were executed during the great persecution of 1866.

3. Haemi Martyrdom Holy Grounds

A rare lowland fortress, these walls were where about 1,000 Catholics were martyred during the great persecution of 1866. The Yeosutgol Holy Site, containing relics from the martyred, is located nearby.

4. Chungdong First Methodist Church

This lovely Victorian Gothic church near Seoul's Deoksugung Palace was founded in 1898, making it Korea's oldest Protestant church.

5. Seung Dong Presbyterian Church

Built in the early 20th century, this massive brick church in Seoul's Insa-dong district played a vital role in the Korean struggle for independence from Japanese colonial rule.

6. Seoul Anglican Cathedral

Just behind Deoksugung Palace, Seoul Anglican Cathedral is not only one of the most beautiful churches in Seoul, but one of the finest pieces of Romanesque architecture in East Asia.

7. Ganghwa Anglican Cathedral

Built by a royal carpenter who participated in the reconstruction of Gyeongbokgung Palace, this small church perfectly harmonizes East and West.

6

7

MAP OF 21 RELIGIOUS SITES IN KOREA

7 BUDDHIST TEMPLES

1. **Jogyesa** Jongno-gu, Seoul
2. **Bulguksa** Gyeongju-si, Gyeongsangbuk-do
3. **Buseoksa** Yeongju-si, Gyeongsangbuk-do
4. **Songgwangsa** Suncheon-si, Jeollanam-do
5. **Tongdosa** Yangsan-si, Gyeongsangnam-do
6. **Haeinsa** Hapcheon-gun, Gyeongsangnam-do
7. **Beopjusa** Boeun-gun, Chungcheongbuk-do

7 CONFUCIAN SITES

1. **Jongmyo Shrine** Jongno-gu, Seoul
2. **Seonggyungwan Mumyo Shrine** Jongno-gu, Seoul
3. **Dosan Seowon** Andong-si, Gyeongsangbuk-do
4. **Sosu Seowon** Yeongju-si, Gyeongsangbuk-do
5. **Byeongsan Seowon** Yeongju-si, Gyeongsangbuk-do
6. **Huwon Garden** In Changdeokgung, Jongno-gu, Seoul
7. **Soswaewon Garden** Damnyang-gun, Jeollanam-do

7 CHRISTIAN SITES

1. **Myeong-dong Cathedral** Jung-gu, Seoul
2. **Jeoldusan Martyrs Grounds** Mapo-gu, Seoul
3. **Haemi Martyrdom Holy Grounds** Seosan-si, Chungcheongnam-do
4. **Chungdong First Methodist Church** Jung-gu, Seoul
5. **Seung Dong Presbyterian Church** Jongno-gu, Seoul
6. **Seoul Anglican Cathedral** Jung-gu, Seoul
7. **Ganghwa Anglican Cathedral** Ganghwa-gun, Incheon

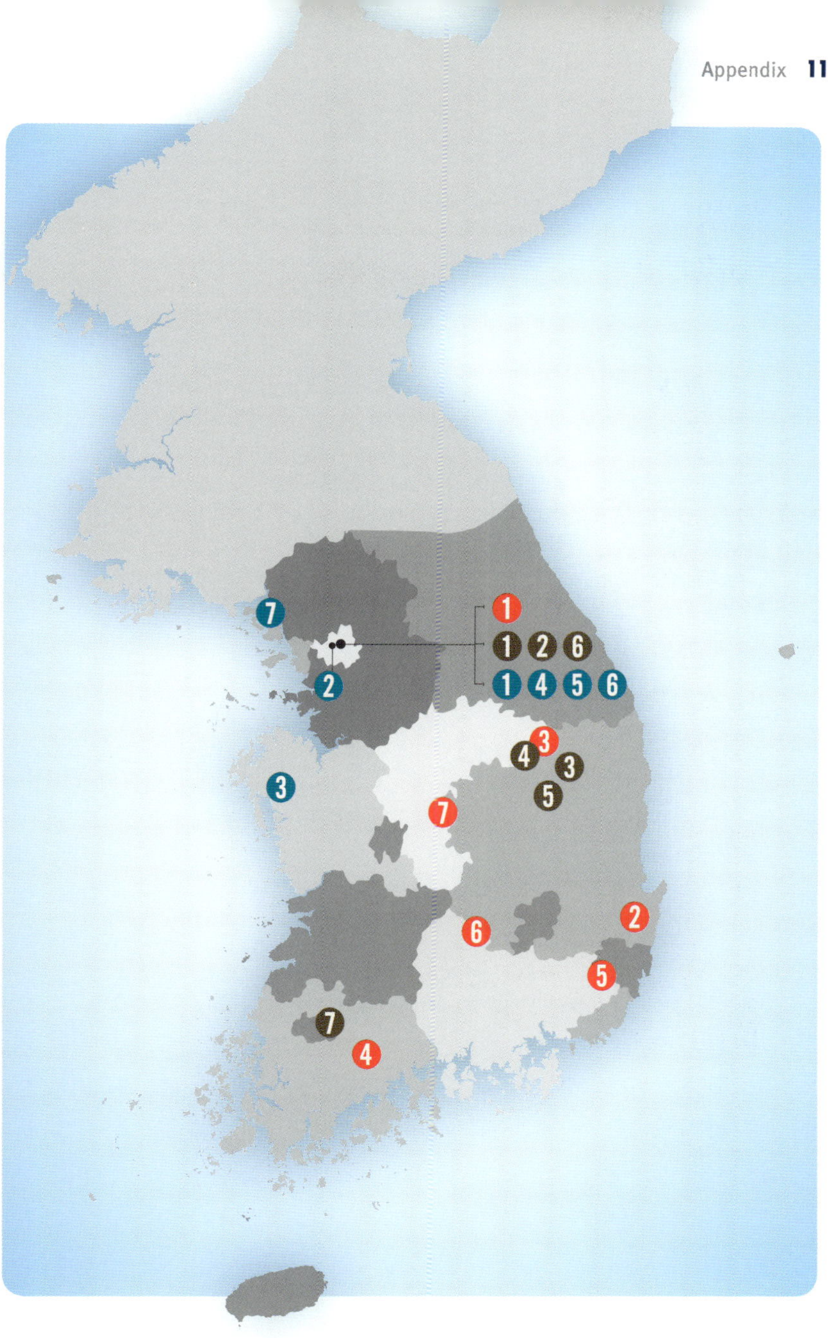
1
1 2 6
1 4 5 6
7
2
3
4
3
3
5
7
2
6
5
7
4

The content of this book has been compiled, edited, and supplemented by Robert Koehler from the following articles published in:

***Koreana* Vol. 6, No. 2, Summer 1992**

"An Interview with Kim Kum-hwa" By Yi Sung-nam

***Koreana* Vol. 24, No. 1, Spring 2010**

"A Tour of Korea's Jongga Museums" by Charles La Shure
"Jongga Ancestral Rituals and Food Culture" by Lee Yeun-ja

***Koreana* Vol. 25, No. 2, Summer 2011**

"Praying for the Mercy of the Goddess of Wind: Yeongdeung Shaman Rites" by Kim Yoo-kyung

***Koreana* Vol. 25, No. 4, Winter 2011**

"After 1,000 Years, Tripitaka Koreana Opens New Era for Buddhist Research" by Lewis Lancaster
"Diverse Festivities Unravel the Woodblocks' Profound" by Charles La Shure

Introduction, Chapter 1, 5, 6, and parts of Chapter 2, 3 and 4 were newly written by Robert Koehler.

PHOTOGRAPHS

Korea Tourism Organization 18, 21, 22, 25, 33, 37, 44, 49, 51, 53, 54~55, 57, 65, 66, 79, 80, 106, 107, 108, 109, 110

Yonhap Photo 4, 5, 7, 8, 10, 11, 13, 14, 15, 16, 17, 18, 20, 23, 24, 25, 26~27, 29, 30, 32, 34, 36, 38, 39, 41, 42, 43, 45, 48, 51, 52, 56, 58~59, 60, 61, 62, 65, 68, 69, 71, 72, 73, 75, 76, 77, 78, 80, 84, 85, 87, 90, 92, 93, 94, 97, 98, 100~101, 102

Robert Koehler 5, 46~47, 61, 83, 88, 89, 91, 95, 106, 108, 111

Gansong Art Museum 14~15

Image Today 4, 12, 74

Credits

Publisher	Kim Hyung-geun
Writer	Robert Koehler
Editor	Jang Woo-jung
Copy Editor	Colin A. Mouat, Daisy Larios
Designer	Min So-young